THE CHRISTIAN'S CALLING

THE CHRISTIAN'S CALLING

Revised Edition

DONALD R. HEIGES

FORTRESS PRESS   **PHILADELPHIA**

Library of Congress Cataloging in Publication Data

Heiges, Donald R.
   The Christian's calling.

   Bibliography: p.
   1. Vocation. I. Title.
   BV4740.H4 1984   248.4   84–47923
   ISBN 0–8006–1795–9 (pbk.)

K953C84   Printed in the United States of America   1–1795

TO MY PARENTS
who walked worthily of the
calling to which they were called

CONTENTS

FOREWORD

The 1958 series of the Knubel-Miller Lectures of the United Lutheran Church in America was the occasion for the publication of the original edition of this book. Five lectures on the subject of "The Christian's Calling" were presented at seven locations from coast to coast. The audiences were mostly made up of Lutherans and, more specifically, Lutheran pastors.

Twenty-five years have come and gone. In 1958, Dwight Eisenhower was President, the country was prosperous, and an era of good feeling prevailed. A quarter of a century ago those who wanted to work could find jobs; today millions who want to work cannot find employment. Then big business was all out for increasing productivity; today big business seems to be more concerned with mergers, plant closures or removals, and tax write-offs. We seem no longer to be in a constantly expanding economy. Nevertheless, there are evidences that we are emerging from an economic depression, but this trend has not dispelled a pervading sense of uneasiness, uncertainty, and even cynicism, especially among the younger generation. Furthermore, twenty-five years ago predated the era of computers and the robotization of industry, which has only deepened the sense of uneasiness, uncertainty, and cynicism. No one can doubt that we live in a different world than it was in 1958.

This revised book takes into account another change both in the American and in the world scene, namely, the phenomenal growth in ecumenical consciousness and cooperation since 1958. Consequently, this edition is no longer addressed only to Lutherans but to an ecumenical readership. For example, whereas the last chapter had been based almost entirely on Lutheran documentation, it is now addressed to members of the household of God conceived as inclusive of many traditions. We have finally discovered that we can really learn from and live with one another even though there are still many differences among the various churches.

Yet, although significant changes have taken place over the past quarter of a century, there is evidence that the mood depicted in the first chapter of the original edition is prevalent in contemporary culture to a large extent. During the spring of 1983 it was my privilege to discuss with five college and university groups of students on as many different campuses the subject of Christian vocation. These students reminded me that they were not around when the original edition of this book was published, but they insisted that the cultural malaise described in the first chapter still characterized the majority of today's students. In fact, the students of one university group reported that the incidence of suicides and attempted suicides was higher today on their campus than it had been for at least forty years. Alienation and meaninglessness are still very much with us today.

For many revisions in this edition the author is indebted to the suggestions and criticisms of his colleagues on the faculty of the Lutheran Theological Seminary at Gettysburg, and for the typing of the manuscript to the Seminary's veteran and highly competent staff member, Ms. Mary Miller.

DONALD R. HEIGES

Eve of All Saints, 1983

1
LIFE WITHOUT VOCATION

I was a kid in 1942 when I got out of art school. I wanted to make a lot of money and become famous. In five years I'll own the world. I'll be in New York driving a Cadillac and owning my own plane. I wanted gold cuff links and babes and the big house in the country. The whole bit. The American Dream. That beautiful, ugly, vicious dream that we all, in some way, have. I wanted to be a key man in industry. Over the years I realized that there isn't any key man—that every man, every human is a commodity to be exploited. And destroyed and cast aside. For thirty years I have been a commercial hack.

The problem isn't the work itself. Does it have a real meaning or is it a piece of commercial pap? The question gets down to who the hell pays for it? You want a living, you want to eat. Say you're a bookkeeper. Are you counting something of human value or are you counting for the Syndicate or for the Pentagon? Are you a bookkeeper counting dead bodies or children at school? What kind of an individual are you? Do you feel you are something because you create a cute commercial spot that sells a product that has no human value? Is it all purely style? Is there no content?[1]

Who is pouring out this bitter complaint? A commercial artist and designer, for whom life and work have turned sour at age fifty. He is a long way from realizing the dream he had when he finished art school, but he has made his share of money, he would be called reasonably successful, he has his own staff of fifteen artists who are quite capable of producing what their clients want and will pay for without quibbling. Furthermore, he seems to be happily married and the father of a devoted family. But he is living completely outside the realm of vocation. Indeed, he probably never heard the word "vocation." Just what is "vocation" anyhow, and what difference could it make in this artist's life and work?

The question comes to the surface in another world of thought and experience. Edwin J. Delattre, president of St. John's College at Annapolis, Maryland, and Santa Fe, New Mexico, is writing in defense of liberal arts education and lodges this protest:

Most students, moreover, are not learning the difference between a vocation and an occupation, between having a calling and having a job. Odd, isn't it, that educational institutions themselves now call training that may, at best, lead to a job "vocational training," as though anything so limited as training, as opposed to education, could prepare a person for a vocation properly understood?

It seems to me unfair to obliterate the distinction between jobs and callings, because it deprives the young of a glimpse of what it is to aspire to a life of fulfillment partly through one's work. "Nothing is so bad for the soul as feeling that it is dispensed on nothing," Walter Lippman observed, and we are not universally teaching the basic concepts by which to guard against lives "dispensed on nothing."[2]

It is encouraging to note that an educator in such a prestigious position as president of St. John's College is both aware of and takes seriously the distinction between job and vocation, especially as this distinction bears upon the relevance of the liberal arts. And he reacts with distaste, if not horror, to human existence that is only job-oriented. But how is "vocation properly understood"? That is the basic question underlying this entire book. President Delattre seems to intimate an understanding that takes into purview all of human existence, including the world of work.

At the moment, however, the quotation Delattre uses from Walter Lippman bears pointedly and poignantly upon this chapter: "Nothing is so bad for the soul as feeling that it is dispensed on nothing." Is that not another way of saying that nothing is so bad for the soul as life without vocation?

The purpose of this book is to explore the meaning of vocation and the difference a sense of vocation makes in the life of a Christian. In the fourth chapter we shall attempt to describe a concept of vocation relevant to the contemporary scene. An examination of vocation in the Bible and in the writings of Martin Luther will help us to understand "vocation." First, however, it is necessary to indicate, at least in an elementary way, what is meant by vocation. This can be done in two simple affirmations: (a) Vocation takes within its sweep the totality of a person's life—not just remunerative employment. (b) Vocation is life lived within the purpose and power of God. At this point we are interested in seeing what happens when life is not lived within God's purpose and power. Specifically, we shall examine work without meaning and then push back the horizons and look upon life without meaning.

What is the Point of Working?

Long ago—thousands of years before supermarkets and assembly lines—the author of Ecclesiastes raised a perennial question: "What has a man from all the toil and strain with which he toils beneath the sun? For all his days are full of pain, and his work is a vexation; even in the night his mind does not rest" (Eccl. 2:22 – 23). Indeed, ever since expulsion from Eden, human beings have known the vexation of toil, but in many areas of contemporary life that vexation has become destructive of the human spirit.

The issue here is not basically one of drudgery. Work can make terrible demands on the body or the mind; it can be dirty, disagreeable, dangerous, deadening, and deafening, and still not be inherently destructive of the human spirit. This is not to say that dirt, disagreeableness, danger, monotony, and noise should not be reduced to a minimum. In this regard we have come a long way since the early days of Western industrialism when women and children as well as men were subjected to bestial treatment in the factories and the mines. But the most serious curse that can befall labor is meaninglessness. Drudgery can be borne within the context of meaning, but when a person sees no point, no meaning, no significance in his toil, then the soul is endangered and the only healthy reaction is one of abandoning the job.

Years ago I heard a story about a gang of laborers digging holes in a street. After they had blasted through six inches of asphalt and concrete with a compressed air hammer, and had shoveled out rock, sand, and soil to a depth of about five feet, the boss inspected the hole and yelled, "Okay, fill 'er up." Then they would move down the street some distance, proceed to dig another hole, and when it was five feet deep the boss would look at it and yell, "Okay, fill 'er up." And so it went on all morning. After lunch the men gathered around the boss and announced: "We quit. Pay us off." The astounded foreman asked if the work was too hard or the pay too low, but the men just shook their heads. Finally, one of them blurted out: "We quit because no one is going to make damn fools of us. Just diggin' holes and fillin' 'em up again!" "Oh," said the boss, "is that it? Well, you see, the records for this old section of the city have been lost, and we're trying to find the water mains." The men went back to work. Human beings want to see some point to what they are doing, even if what they are doing makes no great demands upon the mind or the body.

Robert Michaelsen emphasizes this facet of human nature in his criticism of the classic concept of "the economic man" in industrial development.

> It appears that although much of the approach to the worker—both by industrialists and union leaders—has been guided by the "myth" of "economic man," still the over-all reaction of the worker has demonstrated his basic recognized and unrecognized interest in far more than material reward. He seeks much more out of work than his pay check. He wants some sense of his role in the total enterprise—a feeling that his work means something in itself, and that there is a future in it beyond the tangible financial return. He longs for a place in the industrial community—some satisfaction of his urge as a social individual. Possibly he would also like a fuller voice in the decision-making that takes place in the industrial community, and some sense of responsibility for the condition and use of industrial production. Studies of industrial workers . . . seem to indicate that when the worker feels that he is getting some of these things, he finds meaning and joy in his work almost regardless of economic incentive.[3]

And this is where vocation comes into the picture, because *vocation gives meaning, significance to all of life, including labor.* Obviously there are many possible levels of meaning; vocation is the level of meaning created by God's initiative and action. When vocation disappears from life, sufficient meaning to keep a person going is sometimes found on lower levels—in certain eras, under certain conditions, or in certain occupations. For example, a physician who is an avowed atheist may gain sufficient technical satisfaction from his or her work to keep at it with enduring interest. A case in point is Dr. Lucas Marsh in the novel *Not as a Stranger,* by Morton Thompson.[4]

The tragedy is that the methods of mass production in modern industry do not by and large provide those "certain conditions" necessary to establish meaning on a level lower than that of vocation, and since millions employed in industry have no sense of vocation, toil in itself is devoid of significance. Another story will make this fact unforgettable.

Three Europeans on a tour of industry in the United States were visiting a mammoth manufacturing plant. They stopped to chat with a man operating a machine that turned out a slightly curved piece of metal about five inches long. Here is how the conversation went:

QUESTION: How long have you been working at this machine?

ANSWER: Six years.

QUESTION: Just what are you making?

ANSWER: U273.

QUESTION: Yes, but what is the name of it?

ANSWER: Name? It has no name—just U273.

QUESTION: Well, then, what is U273 for—what purpose does it serve?

ANSWER: What's it for? How should I know?

QUESTION: Why do you keep on making U273?

ANSWER: It pays $7.90 an hour. Hey, are you guys some of them there Communists?

End of conversation. Mass production meaningless? It is so meaningless, and so taken for granted, that if one pushes the question Why? too far, one is liable to be suspected of being subversive.

That much mass production reduces human beings to the status of almost unconscious cogs in machines is no longer disputed. In fact, constant repetition has rendered the charge hackneyed. But its implications must be faced. Persons who are condemned to operate a machine that they do not own, to produce an object labeled U273 to be incorporated into a product that they did not design and that they may never see except in advertisements, for a company to which they do not belong and over which they have no control and from which they may receive a layoff slip at any time—such persons, finding no meaning in their work, either find some significance to their lives elsewhere—in a hobby, commercialized entertainment, family—or they sink more and more deeply into the quicksand of despair.

Industrialists, of course, have not been unaware of this problem. In the words of the chairman of General Foods Corporation: "You can buy a man's time, you can buy a man's physical presence at a given place; you can even buy a measured number of skilled muscular motions per hour or day. But you cannot buy enthusiasm; you cannot buy loyalty; you cannot buy devotion of hearts, minds, and souls."[5] And so industrialists have called in public relations and personnel management experts to solve the problem. As a result, all sorts of gimmicks have been introduced—music piped into factories, intramural sports, counseling services, profit-sharing schemes, etc.—and these have doubtless helped to make the workers less restive with their lot, but it cannot be said that they have solved the basic problem. Furthermore, one gets the impression that these clever personnel management methods are being used to manipulate people rather than being introduced out of a genuine concern for their welfare. In fact, the corporation executive quoted above bluntly states that "the human will to work" is "the most promising single source of *productivity* [*sic*]."

The void that exists in the absence of vocation on the machine level extends also into the higher echelons of the industrial order. "The machine man" of the factories has his counterpart in "the organization man" of the administrative offices, as so strikingly and terrifyingly depicted by William H. Whyte.[6] The latter is chained to the organization just as surely as the former is chained to the machine, except that the person in the factory seldom if ever worships the machine in contrast to the person in the administrative offices who tends to deify the organization. In either case the integrity and the initiative of the individual have almost disappeared.

Depersonalization proceeds apace because, on the one hand, only the machine matters and, on the other hand, only the organization matters. Yet there seems to be this difference: people in the factory are forced to become robots in order to survive, while people in the administrative offices are willing to lose themselves in the organization because they believe this is the right way to get the enormous tasks in the nation done and to realize the primary objectives of their own lives. As Whyte points out,[7] the members of the managerial class seek meaning through community, but commit the fallacy of regarding the organization as community when actually it is merely a form of collectivism.

Reference has been made to "the primary objectives of their own lives," i.e., those of the junior and senior executives. The list is well known: occupational and financial security, recognition in a particular field of competence, social status and perhaps prestige, leisure enough to enjoy "the good things of life," and early retirement in order to continue to enjoy these good things on a full-time basis just as long as possible. In 1957, Phillip E. Jacobs reported[8] that these objectives were being rather well formulated during undergraduate years and were the common property of the majority of the nation's college and university students. In 1980, Arthur Levine in an impressive analysis prepared for the Carnegie Council on Policy Studies in Higher Education discovered that after a quarter of a century the undergraduate mood remained essentially the same except that disillusion about the nation and skepticism about the future had deepened. Both the campus violence and the social idealism of the 1960s and the early 1970s have disappeared. "Meism" today "permeates all aspects of the undergraduate world, from politics to education to social life to the future that students envision."[9]

The following *Time* magazine anecdote reported in its 1951 survey of college student attitudes could well have come out of a similar survey done in 1983:

> On a sunny Sunday not long ago, Sociology Professor Carr B. Lavell of George Washington University took one of his students on a fishing trip. He is a brilliant student, president of his class, a big man on campus, evidently with a bright future in his chosen field, medicine. In the bracing air, professor and student had a quiet talk. Why had he gone into medicine? asked the professor. Answer: medicine looked lucrative. What did he want to do as a doctor? Get into the specialty that offered the biggest fees. Did he think that a doctor owed some special service to the community? Probably not. "I am just like any one else," said the student. "I just want to prepare myself so that I can get the most out of it for me. I hope to make a lot of money in a hurry. I'd like to retire in about ten years and do the things I really want." And what are those? "Oh," said the brilliant student, "fishing, traveling, taking it easy."[10]

Time's allegation that such an orientation to life was typical not only of the great majority of undergraduates but also of those going into the so-called professions in the early 1950s seems to have just as much justification in the early 1980s.

In short, what those in the managerial class of industry want out of life is indistinguishable from what those in the professions seek. A difference is that the former seek these objectives through participation in a managerial collective, whereas the latter seek them primarily on an individualistic basis, although, with reference to the field of medicine for example, the power of collective action through the American Medical Association, the local medical associations, and hospital staffs cannot be overlooked. The fact remains that in both categories the chief ends of life are projected in self-centered and materialistic terms.

This is a glimpse of work today without vocation. I say "a glimpse" advisedly because no attempt has been made to survey the entire occupational field.[11] What has been seen, however, in factory workers, in the managers of industry, and in the professions is indicative of the orientation of almost all work in our culture. Vocation, except as a casual synonym for occupation, has been exiled from the world of toil.

A most disturbing dimension of the workaday world in the 1980s is, however, the brutal fact of massive and, to a large extent, endemic unemployment. In other words, the absence of sufficient work opportunities in our culture is now as threatening as the destructive nature of so many of the existing jobs. In fact, the unemployment rate is the highest it has been in forty years. In California alone it is estimated that more than 200,000 jobs have disappeared within two years. The major causes of this devastation have been cited as the technological revolution sparked by automation, robotization, and computerization; the epidemic number of plant closures and the movement of the plants to foreign countries where labor and other expenses are cheaper; and the shift in emphasis in capital investment from increasing productivity to speculation, mergers, and tax write-offs. Today's vast unemployment is symptomatic of almost imponderable structural changes in the world of work, thus heavily underlining the crucial place of work in any consideration of vocation but not really changing the basic issues involved in its absence.

Attention has been focused on that segment of life known as "work" partly because it is such a large segment of human life and partly because those who still refer occasionally to vocation restrict its applicability to work. Since it is a thesis of this book that vocation encompasses the whole of human existence, it now becomes necessary to take a look at life without vocation.

What Is the Point of Living?

When human beings begin to wrestle with the question, Why work? they are usually not too far removed from a much more devastating question, namely, Why live? If a worker went to a typical personnel department of a corporation with the query, Why work at all? Why human existence and human relations? Why live? he or she would be referred to a psychiatrist, or at least dismissed summarily, because it would appear that the person is dangerously close to going off the deep end. And indeed that person is close to the deep end—the deep end of meaninglessness.

Of course, this problem is not unique to our times. Individuals have doubtless struggled with it since the dawn of self-consciousness. The author of Ecclesiastes, who has already been quoted, is one of these individuals. He writes:

> I have seen everything that is done under the sun; and behold, all is vanity and a striving after wind. What is crooked cannot be made straight, and what

is lacking cannot be numbered. . . . For of the wise man as of the fool there is no enduring remembrance, seeing that in the days to come all will have been long forgotten. How the wise man dies just like the fool! So I hated life, because what is done under the sun was grievous to me; for all is vanity and a striving after wind. . . . So I turned about and gave my heart up to despair (Eccl. 1:14 – 15; 2:16 – 18, 20).

Yes, in every generation there have been individuals overwhelmed with the sense of futility. But periodically in the course of human history whole cultures seem to become infected with the virus of meaninglessness. This appears to be true today of the culture of the West. Obviously the disease is not as advanced in some sections of Western culture as in others, but evidences of the virus appear almost everywhere.

Many of our poets, novelists, dramatists, philosophers, and theologians have been preoccupied for most of this century with the anatomy of meaninglessness. A few samples of this literature will provide a background for consideration of the problem at hand. These samplings can best be understood as footnotes to the morphology of despair, succinctly stated by the late Joseph Fort Newton in these words: "When a man loses faith in God, he worships humanity; when faith in humanity fails, he worships science, as so many are trying to do today. When faith in science fails, man worships himself, and at the altar of his own idolatry he receives a benediction of vanity. Hence the tedious egotism of our day, when men are self-centered and self-obsessed, unable to get themselves out of their own hands."[12]

T. S. Eliot was among the first of twentieth-century English writers to depict modern man stripped of meaning. His poem *The Waste Land* has been cited by almost every diagnostician of our cultural malaise—and deservedly. The aimlessness, the emptiness, the aridness of life has seldom been so powerfully portrayed.

> Here is no water but only rock
> Rock and no water and the sandy road
> The road winding above among the mountains
> Which are mountains of rock without water
> If there were water we should stop and drink
> Amongst the rock one cannot stop or think
> Sweat is dry and feet are in the sand
> If there were only water amongst the rock
> Dead mountain mouth of carious teeth that cannot spit

Here one can neither stand nor lie nor sit
There is not even silence in the mountains
But dry sterile thunder without rain
There is not even solitude in the mountains
But red sullen faces sneer and snarl
From doors of mud cracked houses
                        If there were water
And no rock
If there were rock
And also water
And water
A spring
A pool among the rock
If there were the sound of water only
Not the cicada
And dry grass singing
But sound of water over a rock
Where the hermit-thrush sings in the pine trees
Drip drop drip drop drop drop drop
But there is no water[13]

The imagery is so biblical through and through that scores of passages, especially from the prophets, come to mind, as, for example, this from Jeremiah (2:12 – 13): "Be appalled, O heavens, at this, be shocked, be utterly desolate, says the Lord, for my people have committed two evils: they have forsaken me, the fountain of living waters, and hewed out cisterns for themselves, broken cisterns, that can hold no water."

Symbolism is replaced by conceptualization in the first chorus from Eliot's "The Rock," but the mood is similar to that of *The Waste Land*—an aching sense of something missing, the one thing needful.

The endless cycle of idea and action,
Endless invention, endless experiment,
Brings knowledge of motion, but not of stillness;
Knowledge of speech, but not of silence;
Knowledge of words, and ignorance of the Word.
All our knowledge brings us nearer to our ignorance,
All our ignorance brings us nearer to death,
But nearness to death no nearer to GOD.
Where is the Life we have lost in living?
Where is the wisdom we have lost in knowledge?
Where is the knowledge we have lost in information?[14]

Knowledge of words, and ignorance of the Word—this is the plight of contemporary humanity in its wasteland.

In our disrupted world we well know what "displaced persons" are—those people driven or self-exiled from their homelands who wander over the face of the earth. Today this is the spiritual state of millions of men and women—displaced persons, homeless in the cosmos and homeless among their own kind, with nowhere to lay their heads, nowhere to rest their souls. Spokesman for the displaced souls is Franz Kafka, who has been described as "the most representative figure in twentieth-century literature." In fact, W. H. Auden goes so far as to say: "Had one to name the artist who comes nearest to bearing the same kind of relation to our age that Dante, Shakespeare, and Goethe bore to theirs, Kafka is the first we would think of."[15] He is the writer par excellence of alienation.

To a greater or lesser degree, creative literature is always autobiographical, but this was especially true of Kafka. In laying his own soul bare he laid bare the souls of his contemporaries. "I have been forty years wandering from Canaan. . . . It is indeed a kind of wandering in the wilderness in reverse that I am undergoing."[16] As J. Hillis Miller points out, for Kafka "the entire human community is in the desert, attempting to build an impious tower of Babel to scale heaven, but really cutting itself off more and more from God and creating a self-enclosed structure of purely human values and institutions. . . . Once, long ago, as Kafka says in one of his very last stories, the Word was close to man, and interpenetrated his world, but now it has withdrawn altogether, and all mankind is lost."[17] The imagery of the desert reminds one of Eliot's *The Waste Land*. Kafka describes his own condition (and therefore the condition of every person) in terms of dryness, of being deprived of water. He finds the "well gone dry, water at an unattainable depth and no certainty it is there."[18]

One of the most horrible stories written by Kafka is "The Metamorphosis."[19] Gregor Samsa, an undistinguished traveling salesman, becomes so alienated from his community and his family that he wakes up one morning to discover that he has been transformed into an enormous cockroach. This amazing event makes his alienation complete. His "human" consciousness remains, but the ability to communicate with his family is completely gone. Physically he shares the same house (locked in his own room or released now and then to look at the family scene), but he could just as well have been a million miles away from his father and mother and sister, because there is no way to let them know his thoughts. In his excruciating agony the only escape is death, but, unlike Willie Loman in J. Arthur Miller's play *The Death of a Salesman*,[20] he cannot destroy himself. His fate is to die slowly, until at the last little more remains than the dry shell and emptiness within.

But humankind's alienation is basically vertical, not merely horizontal. Kafka calls attention not only to people's isolation from others but also to their isolation from the ground of their being. In other words, Gregor Samsa's haunting concern was the God-relationship which he knew only negatively as something necessary but not realizable. "There is a goal, but no way; what we call the way is only wavering."[21] In his despair and frustration he charges that original sin, supposedly committed by man against God, was actually "committed upon him."[22]

According to Kafka, deep down in the memory of each individual cast adrift on the void of the contemporary world is a picture of human existence characterized by ordered relationships, by a structure in which the individual once had a niche to fill. The fleeting perception of such a picture merely deepens the person's nostalgia, alienation, frustration; it does not provide a cue to the resolution of his or her predicament. Here is Kafka's description of life without vocation as sensed by modern people:

> He was once part of a monumental group. Round some elevated figure or other in the center were ranged in carefully thought-out order symbolical images of the military caste, the arts, the sciences, the handicrafts. He was one of those many figures. Now the group is long since dispersed, or at least he has left it and makes his way through life alone. He no longer has even his old vocation, indeed he has actually forgotten what he once represented. Probably it is the very forgetting that gives rise to a certain melancholy, uncertainty, unrest, a certain longing for vanished ages, darkening the present.[23]

Then there is Jean-Paul Sartre, who cannot be passed by in any consideration of the blight of futility. Whatever else may be said about this controversial figure, it must be affirmed that Sartre is the master at depicting human beings who are trapped, not as people are trapped in cheap westerns and detective stories but trapped by the very nature of life itself. On the one hand, Sartre denies that there are any meanings anywhere except those which human beings create; on the other hand, in all his writings, philosophical or otherwise, he implies a givenness, if not a structure, to existence which is forever defeating persons and their meanings. Meanings and values are therefore fragile, tentative, arbitrary, precarious. Although

Sartre affirms self-consciousness and the freedom of consciousness to create meanings, he insists that there would be no consciousness if it were not for the world outside consciousness. Between consciousness and the external world there is a sharp cleft which can never be overcome. And since the external world includes other objects endowed with consciousness and freedom, namely, other persons, alienation is deepest on the human level because the most formidable threat to a person is a person, not a thing. Only another person can penetrate my consciousness, thereby limiting, perhaps perverting, and even destroying me.

All this can be seen in Sartre's play *No Exit.* Two women and a man are ushered one by one into a stuffy Victorian room, and the realization gradually comes that they are in hell. Inez admits at once that she is in the "right" place, but Estelle and Garcin try to pose as misplaced persons. Eventually their defenses are destroyed and each stands naked before the other. Then they begin to wonder when the torturer will come, and what form the torture will take. As they wait, they begin to irritate each other as if by an inexorable compulsion. Estelle's earthly desires continue unabated; Inez is hard and brittle—"a dead twig, ready for the burning"; but Garcin died a coward, and this ignominy he can't shake off. As the mutual bedeviling mounts to the point of violence, Garcin makes a wild attempt to crash the bolted door, but there is NO EXIT. As they face the fact that there is no escape from each other, the horrible truth becomes clear—their torture consists in their condemnation to torture each other forever and ever and ever, and they break out in the laughter of the damned. As Garcin summarizes their situation, the reader perceives that this is Sartre's summary of the human situation, per se: "So this is hell. I'd never have believed it. You remember all we were told about the torture-chambers, the fire and brimstone, the 'burning marl.' Old wives' tales! There's no need for red-hot pokers. *Hell is—other people!*"[24] (Italics mine.)

The atheism of Sartre is primarily an inference from his view of humankind whose glory as well as whose damnation is freedom. There is not a more stalwart defender of human liberty than Sartre. Self-consciousness is freedom to make decisions, even though many decisions are nullified by external circumstances. To posit God as Determiner of Destiny would be to endanger human freedom, and this Sartre resolutely refuses to do—but not without a discernible wistfulness. For an individual in his or her decision-making has no guides, no norms, no standards, and only the abyss below. Sartre finds it "very distressing that God does not exist, because all possibility of finding values in a heaven of ideas disappears along with Him; there can no longer be an *a priori* good, since there is no infinite and perfect consciousness to think it." The "forlornness" of human beings is rooted in their recognition "that God does not exist and that [they] have to face all the consequences of this."[25]

And what appears in the consciousness of a person who, having exercised decision-making liberty in a godless world, stands at the brink of death? Listen to Pablo, the principal character in Sartre's short story entitled "The Wall," as he reflects upon his predicament during the night preceding his scheduled execution at dawn: "At that moment I felt that I had my whole life in front of me and I thought, 'It's a damned lie.' It was worth nothing because it was finished. . . . I had spent my time counterfeiting eternity, I had understood nothing. . . . Death had disenchanted everything."[26] In his reflection upon his fate, Pablo's isolation is absolute. As Ignazio Silone so well says: "He who has faith is never alone. But the atheist is always alone, even if from morning to night he lives in crowded streets. The soul that does not know God is a leaf detached from the tree, a single, solitary leaf, that falls to the ground, dries up, and rots."[27]

Such is the bleak prospect of life without essential meaning (i.e., without God) as depicted by Eliot (from the perspective of the Christian faith), by Kafka (from the perspective of the residual religiousness of renounced Judaism), and by Sartre (from the perspective of declared atheism). It is a prospect envisioned by Nietzsche, who as early as 1882 wrote: "Is there any up or down left? Are we not straying as through an infinite nothing? Do we not feel the breath of empty space? Has it not become colder? Is not night and more night coming on all the while? Must not lanterns be lit in the morning?"[28] It is a prospect expressed succinctly by the Russian poet Tiutchev:

> Behold man, without home,
> orphaned, alone, impotent,
> facing the dark abyss;
> all light and life
> are no more than a past dream, far away.
> And in this strange mysterious night
> he sees and knows a fatal heritage.[29]

What does this prospect have to do with vocation? Just this: Only when human beings believe in God can they perceive substantial meaning in existence; only when they can perceive meaning can they be captivated by vocation; and when they are captivated by vocation, they can live above despair to the glory of God.

It should be noted, however, that no attempt is being made to defend the thesis that the contemporary phenomenon of meaninglessness can be explained simply in terms of the decay of a dynamic concept of vocation. The roots of meaninglessness are deep, diverse, and devious. What is being affirmed is that the Christian understanding of vocation is tremendously relevant to the problem of meaninglessness in culture as a whole, in commerce and industry, in other occupational fields, and in community relationships. The picture painted by Eliot, Kafka, and Sartre probably appears extravagant to average Americans, but they certainly recognize some evidences of meaninglessness around them and within their own lives—at least enough to appreciate the thrust of the epigram attributed to Toyohiko Kagawa.

> I read
> In a book
> That a man called
> Christ
> Went about doing good.
> It is very disconcerting to me
> That I am so easily
> Satisfied
> With just
> Going about—

Just going about—that is life without vocation. And that is a far cry from what God the Father of our Lord Jesus intended human life to be.

When "just going about" becomes a burden to people, sometimes they perceive that their only way out is to keep an Appointment. This seems to be the meaning, or at least one of the meanings, of Samuel Beckett's controversial play, *Waiting for Godot.*[30] The principal characters, Vladimir and Estragon, have a vague sense that there is an Appointment which they must keep, and so they wander around aimlessly waiting for Godot. As they wait they hear a cry for help from a chance wayfarer. Vladimir feels a tug to respond. "It is not every day that we are needed. Not indeed that we personally are needed," he says to Estragon. "Let us make the most of it, before it is too late!" But they do not go to the help of Pozzo. Somehow they are powerless to respond until Godot comes. As they sink into a stupor of boredom and frustration, Vladimir soliloquizes:

> To-morrow, when I wake, or think I do, what shall I say of to-day? That with Estragon my friend, at this place, until the fall of night, I waited for Godot? That Pozzo passed, with his carrier, and that he spoke to us? Probably. But in all that what truth will there be? (*Estragon, having struggled with his boots in vain, is dozing off again. Vladimir looks at him.*) He'll know nothing. He'll tell me about the blows he received and I'll give him a carrot. (*Pause.*) . . . But habit is a great deadener. (*He looks again at Estragon.*) At me too someone is looking, of me too someone is saying, He is sleeping, he knows nothing, let him sleep on.[31]

Indeed, Someone is looking at Everyman, but not saying, "sleep on." On the contrary, Someone is calling Everyman to waken from that stupor of boredom, or of meaningless wandering, to a new life swept clean by his Spirit and empowered with a mission to fulfill in his kingdom.

2
VOCATION ACCORDING TO THE SCRIPTURES

Our exploration of the meaning of vocation must begin with the Bible. There is no other place to begin. As everyone knows, the Bible can be quoted to establish almost any point of view, to prove almost any proposition. This feat can be accomplished either by design or by inadvertence simply by quoting out of context or by dealing with only a segment of the biblical material. In our search for the meaning of vocation, we shall attempt to see the Bible "steadily" and to see it "whole."

According to the Scriptures, vocation is basically corporate. God calls a people. In the Old Testament this people, this community, is Israel; in the New Testament, this people, this community is the church. The corporate vocation of the people of God is the context within which an individual is called, has a vocation.

In the Old Testament the Hebrew *qahal* is used to designate the assembly or the congregation of Israel, i.e., the people whom God has summoned or called together for his service. The Septuagint usually translates *qahal* into the Greek *ekklesia*, which originally had the purely secular meaning of the summoned citizenry but to which the Septuagint gave a definitely religious connotation. The early Christians, in turn, took over the word *ekklesia* to designate those called into fellowship with Christ, i.e., the church. The root of *ekklesia* is the noun *klesis*, meaning the call or the calling, and the verb *kalein*, meaning to call or to summon. The Hebrew *qahal*, then, and the Greek *ekklesia* convey the idea of a people summoned or called for a particular purpose. The summons may be in terms of a call to fellowship or feasting, to a task or a responsibility, to a judgment or an accounting. *Klesis* therefore has connotations of joy, of labor, and of discipline.

Vocation in the Old Testament

The theme of the drama of the Old Testament is "God and His People." There are only two major roles, that of God and that of Israel. God, being

God, always knows his lines; but Israel, being finite and sinful, forgets its lines and must be prompted constantly from the wings of the stage of history. The prompters are the "judges," the priests, and the prophets—especially the prophets.

A synopsis of the drama might read as follows: God, who has a purpose he wishes to achieve, calls a people into existence to carry out his purpose. He begins millennia ago by making a covenant with Abraham; by renewing it with Isaac and with Jacob; and finally by sealing it with the self-conscious community of Israel after the deliverance of his people from oppression. The One who calls Israel to be his own possession among all the peoples, a kingdom of priests and a holy nation (Exod. 19:5 – 6), is the One who liberated it from slavery. His purpose is, through Israel, to bless all the inhabitants of the earth. Within the community of Israel each person has a responsibility to perform, whether it be that of king or soldier or craftsman or shepherd. From time to time God calls men and women from their ordinary responsibilities to carry out special missions on behalf of his people. And so Hosea is called from farming to remind Israel of its unfaithfulness, Isaiah from court duties to warn the Kingdom of Judah against foreign entanglements, and Jeremiah from his priestly family obligations to lay upon the people of Jerusalem the demands of righteousness as over against the futility of formalized religion. Despite the faithfulness of God to the covenant, Israel's persistent unfaithfulness leads to disaster after disaster, until only a remnant remains. Out of this remnant, which still remembers the vocation of Israel, eventually comes the Messiah. Let us take a look at some of the detail of this drama.

1. *It is God, the Lord of history, who takes the necessary steps to lay the foundations of a community with a unique destiny.*

Israel pushed back its covenant relationship to the era of the patriarchs. God summons Abram in Haran, and makes a covenant with him: "Go . . . and I will bless you, and . . . I will bless those who bless you . . . and by you all the families of the earth shall bless themselves" (Gen. 12:1 – 3). He renews the covenant with Isaac: "I will multiply your descendants . . . and by your descendants all the nations of the earth shall bless themselves: because Abraham obeyed my voice and kept my charge" (Gen. 26:4 – 5). He renews the covenant with Jacob: "I am the Lord, the God of Abraham your father and the God of Isaac . . . and by you and your descendants shall all the families of the earth bless themselves. Behold, I am with you and will keep you wherever you go" (Gen. 28:13 – 15; cf.

35:10 – 12 and 46:2 – 4). Although the divine summons is here addressed to individuals, the emphasis is upon the continuing people of God and their role among all the families of the earth. The saga of Abraham, Isaac, and Jacob is of the nature of a prologue to the main action of the drama.

At every step the initiative rests with God. Abraham does not, for example, after due reflection, devise and promote a five-hundred-year plan whereby his descendants would greatly prosper and would shape the course of history. Rather, God lays hold of his people, issues orders, and demands obedience; and his people respond in trust.

2. *Through rescue and discipline God creates a community conscious of and dedicated to a unique destiny.*

Until the delivery from bondage in Egypt the people of Israel have no sense of high destiny. Although some sense of destiny can be attributed to the patriarchs, one gets the impression that it was not shared by their numerous offspring and their respective families. And certainly there is no evidence of a sense of high destiny among the oppressed Hebrew slaves under the whips of their Egyptian taskmasters. A dramatic rescue and re-creation had to take place, and for this purpose God called Moses to a special mission.

The call of Moses is one of the classic accounts in the Old Testament of human reaction to divine summons (Exodus 3—4). First, something had to happen to break the thread of routine experience before Moses decided to "turn aside." Only after he had turned aside to gaze at the burning bush could he hear the voice, "Moses, Moses," to which he replied, "Here am I." And the voice continued: "I am the God of your father, the God of Abraham, the God of Isaac, and the God of Jacob. . . . I have seen the affliction of my people who are in Egypt . . . and I have come down to deliver them. . . . Come, I will send you to Pharaoh that you may bring forth my people, the sons of Israel, out of Egypt." Instead of feeling himself highly honored, Moses is dismayed and offers all sorts of excuses: I have no credentials; no one will believe me; I am not a good speaker. Only after every objection has been answered does Moses capitulate.

Interesting and significant as the call of Moses may be, its significance is only derivative. The primary call is the summons to Israel. "When Israel was a child, I loved him, and out of Egypt I called my son" (Hos. 11:1; cf. Exod. 4:22 – 23). God called Israel out of Egypt through Moses. The divine objective was the deliverance of Israel, not the deliverance of Moses from the tedium of sheep-grazing for his father-in-law!

We cannot retell here the story of Israel's deliverance from Egypt and the discipline in the desert. For our purposes it is sufficient to note that the biblical account of those forty years throws much light upon the Hebrew concept of vocation. Out of long and bitter experience Israel's understanding of its vocation was developed and strengthened. One of the finest descriptions of this vocation is in Deuteronomy:

> You are a people holy to the Lord your God; the Lord your God has chosen you to be a people for his own possession, out of all the peoples that are on the face of the earth. It was not because you were more in number than any other people that the Lord set his love upon you and chose you, for you were the fewest of all peoples; but it is because the Lord loves you, and is keeping the oath which he swore to your fathers, that the Lord has brought you out with a mighty hand, and redeemed you from the house of bondage, from the hand of Pharoah king of Egypt (Deut. 7:6 – 8).

At Sinai the covenant is spelled out on the human side in the magnificent and ageless terms of the Decalogue (Exod. 20:1 – 17; cf. Deut. 5:6 – 21). It is to be noted that these obligations of Israel were not determined around a bargaining table with the Senior Member of the covenant, but were the conditions prescribed by the Lord, who said in effect: If I am to be your God and you are to be my people, you cannot do this and this and this. Or to put it positively: "And now, Israel, what does the Lord your God require of you, but to fear the Lord your God, to walk in all his ways, to love him, to serve the Lord your God with all your heart and with all your soul, and to keep the commandments and statutes of the Lord" (Deut. 10:12 – 13; cf. also vs. 14 – 22).

In the biblical account of the forty years in the desert there is the recognition that within the vocation of Israel are not only the special tasks of a Moses or an Aaron but also the special tasks of craftsmen. The instructions for the building of the tabernacle and its equipment contain such illuminating passages as the following:

> The Lord said to Moses, "See, I have called by name Bezalel the son of Uri, son of Hur, of the tribe of Judah: and I have filled him with the Spirit of God, with ability and intelligence, with knowledge and all craftsmanship, to devise artistic designs, to work in gold, silver, and bronze, in cutting stones for setting, and in carving wood, for work in every craft. And behold, I have appointed with him Oholiab, the son of Ahisamach, of the tribe of Dan; and I have given to all able men ability, that they may make all that I have commanded you" (Exod. 31:1 – 6; cf. 35:30 – 35).

"And all women who had ability spun with their hands, and brought what they had spun in blue and purple and scarlet stuff and fine twined linen; all the women whose hearts were moved with ability spun the goats' hair" (Exod. 35:25 – 26). It is to be noted that these men and women practiced their crafts in the ordinary day-by-day life of the community, but here they are being called to special tasks to help advance the spiritual life of the people by the provision of a sanctuary.

The covenant with Israel involved both corporate and individual responsibilities. It is significant that the Decalogue was addressed to Israel as a community but the response of obedience involved the individual members of the community. In other words, the call of Israel placed upon every Israelite the obligation of playing his or her proper role in the consecrated community, of dedicating one's whole being to the service of Israel's God. To which tasks individual members of the community should give themselves, however, was not a matter of special divine revelation. It is true that in the case of the priesthood the whole tribe of Levi was set aside for this purpose (Num. 1:47 – 50; cf. 8:14ff.). Otherwise, variable tribal traditions and the possession of certain skills apparently determined the occupations that the Israelites followed and that provided their tithes and offerings to the Lord. The element of personal choice was probably very small indeed, and of course nonexistent in conscription for the army and for certain other types of service to the nation.

Although there is no evidence that shepherds and carpenters and masons felt themselves to be divinely called to those particular occupations, it was generally recognized that success in all labor depended ultimately upon the divine favor. As the psalmist puts it:

> Unless the Lord builds the house,
>   those who build it labor in vain.
> Unless the Lord watches over the city,
>   the watchman stays awake in vain.
>   (Ps. 127:1)

This passage affirms not only the futility of toil without the divine blessing but also the active involvement of God in human labor. God himself is a worker who directly accomplishes his purposes (e.g., in the creation of the world) or who achieves his purposes through human workers. Therefore, it is important in undertaking any task to seek the divine favor.

> Let the favor of the Lord our God be upon us,

and establish thou the work of our hands upon us,
yea, the work of our hands establish thou it.
                                                        (Ps. 90:17)

All this is true for the routine, ongoing life of the community and of the individuals in the community. Nevertheless, as we have already seen, God may and does call individuals to perform special missions for him. In these cases the individuals are taken away from their routine occupations, where presumably they are already in the service of God, and given unusual assignments. The individuals in these cases are clearly aware that God has explicitly called them in a way he has never before called them.

3. *God raises up the prophets to give "vocational guidance" to his people in the hope that Israel will fulfill its destiny.*

After its Egyptian deliverance and its schooling in the desert, a self-conscious and self-confident Israel under the leadership of Joshua invaded "the Promised Land," and by a slow and painful process sufficiently subdued the inhabitants to superimpose on the land an alien culture. The rough and frequently chaotic years prior to the crowning of David show little evidence of high destiny. Then dawned the brief but golden era of David and Solomon, followed by the tragic splitting of the community into the Northern and Southern Kingdoms, the destruction of the Northern and then of the Southern capital, the exile, and the never fully successful attempt at reconstruction and restoration.

Throughout this checkered story of Israel in the Promised Land are heard the voices of the prophets reminding the people of God of their high calling, pleading with the chosen ones to be faithful in their covenant relationship with him who chose them, warning the elect of their special vulnerability to catastrophe, pointing the way to reform before the day of wrath descended. In the end these valiant attempts to give Israel vocational guidance failed, but the residue of the prophetic utterances delineates the Hebraic concept of calling with profundity and pathos. A sampling of these utterances gives vivid reality to the concept.

Amos (760–746 B.C.), a Judean shepherd, speaks to the Northern Kingdom during the reign of Jeroboam II:

Hear this word that the Lord has spoken against you, O people of Israel, against the whole family which I brought up out of the land of Egypt:
"You only have I known
    of all the families of the earth;

therefore I will punish you
for all your iniquities."
(Amos 3:1 – 2)
I hate, I despise your feasts,
and I take no delight in your solemn assemblies.
Even though you offer me your burnt offerings and cereal offerings,
I will not accept them,
and the peace offerings of your fatted beasts
I will not look upon.
Take away from me the noise of the songs;
to the melody of your harps I will not listen.
But let justice roll down like waters,
and righteousness like an everflowing stream.
(Amos 5:21 – 24)

Hosea (746 – 743 B.C.), following Amos, also condemns Israel in terms of its unfaithfulness to the God who loved Israel and ransomed Israel out of slavery.

Rejoice not, O Israel!
Exult not like the peoples;
for you have played the harlot, forsaking your God.
You have loved a harlot's hire
upon all threshing floors.
(Hos. 9:1)
My God will cast them off,
because they have not hearkened to him;
they shall be wanderers among the nations.
(Hos. 9:17)

Micah (739 – 701 B.C.), a man of the people, denounces both kingdoms for claiming God's protection without meeting the demands of justice.

Hear this, you heads of the house of Jacob
and rulers of the house of Israel,
who abhor justice
and pervert all equity,
who build Zion with blood
and Jerusalem with wrong.
Its heads give judgment for a bribe,
its priests teach for hire,
its prophets divine for money;

yet they lean upon the Lord and say,
   "Is not the Lord in the midst of us?
   No evil shall come upon us."
Therefore because of you
   Zion shall be plowed as a field;
Jerusalem shall become a heap of ruins,
   and the mountain of the house a wooded height.
                  (Mic. 3:9 – 12)

Isaiah (739 – 701 B.C.), a member of the aristocracy, delivers warnings to Judah to eschew foreign alliances and to take God seriously as its only counselor and protector.

"Woe to the rebellious children," says the Lord,
   "who carry out a plan, but not mine;
and who make a league, but not of my spirit,
   that they may add sin to sin;
who set out to go down to Egypt,
   without asking for my counsel,
to take refuge in the protection of Pharaoh,
   and to seek shelter in the shadow of Egypt!"
                  (Isa. 30:1 – 2)

Hear, O heavens, and give ear, O earth;
   for the Lord has spoken:
"Sons have I reared and brought up,
   but they have rebelled against me.
The ox knows its owner,
   and the ass its master's crib;
but Israel does not know,
   my people does not understand."
                  (Isa. 1:2 – 3)

Jeremiah (625 – 586 B.C.), after the collapse of the Northern Kingdom, pleads in vain with Jerusalem to avoid a similar fate, but foresees a saving remnant and a new covenant.

Hear the word of the Lord, O nations,
   and declare it in the coastlands afar off;
say, "He who scattered Israel will gather him,
   and will keep him as a shepherd keeps his flock."
                  (Jer. 31:10)

> Behold, the days are coming, says the Lord, when I will make a new cove-
> nant with the house of Israel and the house of Judah, not like the covenant
> which I made with their fathers when I took them by the hand to bring them
> out of the land of Egypt, my covenant which they broke, though I was their
> husband, says the Lord. But this is the covenant which I will make with the
> house of Israel after those days, says the Lord: I will put my law within them,
> and I will write it upon their hearts; and I will be their God, and they shall be
> my people. (Jer. 31:31 – 33)

To recapitulate the vocational guidance as addressed to Israel by the
prophets: God called you into a covenant relationship with himself to the
end that through you all people would be blessed; this call conferred no
immunity to difficulties or even to disaster in case you failed to keep the
covenant; and so your unfaithfulness has brought punishment, designed
for your purification; out of this crucible of fire a remnant will be saved,
through which God's purposes will yet be realized.

Within the vocation of Israel the prophets were called to perform their
special assignments, just as Moses had received a special call. In the Old
Testament "the call experience" of these persons is at times only intimated
and at other times described in detail. With reference to the latter category, the stories of the call of Moses (Exodus 3—4), of Samuel (1 Samuel
3), of Isaiah (ch. 6), and of Jeremiah (ch. 1) are well known. It is important
to remember that these calls were not sought. In fact, they came as a
surprise, indeed as a shock. Protestations of incompetence were met with
assurances of divine help adequate to the assignment. These calls to special
assignments were not regarded as a summons to greatness (i.e., to honor
and acclaim) but rather to humble service. The carrying out of the special
assignments usually plunged a person into both inner torment and out-
ward persecution at the hands of those being served. Despite the torment
and the abuse, however, there was no escaping such a call from the Holy
One of Israel (cf. Ezek. 33:7 – 9 and the experience of Jonah).

This last observation is equally applicable to Israel itself. God laid his
hand upon Israel to be his very own. In the long story of its vicissitudes,
time and again Israel would have been glad to renounce its election. Israel
tried turning a deaf ear to the divine summons, but to no avail (cf. Jer.
7:12 – 14 and Isa. 65:12). And so divine decimation would follow hard
upon Israel's sin but never to its complete obliteration. Israel could be
carried into captivity, but even there could not escape its divine Pursuer.

Such is the nature of vocation in the Old Testament: the calling of Israel to be God's people for the fulfillment of his purposes in the world. This is the key to the meaning of history and to the meaning of human existence itself. The call of God is both a wondrous and an awesome thing. To be called is to come face to face with great promise and with great peril. To respond in trust and obedience is possible only by the grace of him who calls.

Vocation in the New Testament

Jeremiah and Isaiah saw Israel reduced to a mere "remnant," to which was entrusted the world's only remaining hope. Out of this remnant came the Messiah, in whom were concentrated all the promises God had made to the chosen people. In the words of the Magnificat,

> He has helped his servant Israel,
> in remembrance of his mercy,
> as he spoke to our fathers,
> to Abraham and to his posterity for ever.
> (Luke 1:54 – 55)

The culmination of the ancient promises is also affirmed in the Benedictus.

> Lord, now lettest thou thy servant depart in peace,
> according to thy word;
> for mine eyes have seen thy salvation
> which thou hast prepared in the presence of all peoples,
> a light for revelation to the Gentiles,
> and for glory to thy people Israel.
> (Luke 2:29 – 32)

The fact that Jesus chose twelve disciples (after the twelve tribes) at the outset of his ministry indicates that he deliberately intended to show the continuity between Israel's mission and his mission, and that he saw his mission in relation to a community identified with him. Although he did not specifically use the term "remnant," it is clear that he saw his disciples as the nucleus of a New Israel. "Fear not, little flock [remnant?], for it is your Father's good pleasure to give you the kingdom" (Luke 12:32).

After Pentecost the Christian community claimed explicitly to be the true Israel, the inheritor of all the promises made to the patriarchs. The outpouring of the Spirit is the fulfillment of the prophecy of Joel (Acts 2:17 – 21), and Jesus is vindicated as Israel's Messiah by the resurrection

(Acts 2:36). All who repent and are baptized shall receive the blessing promised "to you and to your children and to all that are far off, every one whom the Lord our God calls to him" (Acts 2:39). "You are the sons of the prophets and of the covenant which God gave to your fathers, saying to Abraham, 'And in your posterity shall all the families of the earth be blessed'" (Acts 3:25). The call of God, however, was still addressed primarily to the Jews, as was the case with the teaching and healing ministry of the Messiah himself. It can be said that at the outset both Jesus and his disciples regarded their mission as being first "to the lost sheep of the house of Israel" (Matt. 10:6).

The God who had promised his blessing to Gentiles through Abraham designated Jesus to be a "light for revelation to the Gentiles" (Luke 2:32). Hence, Paul declared that the call of God was now addressed to all people everywhere, both Jews and Gentiles. The rejection of the gospel by the majority in Israel and its acceptance by a Jewish "remnant" (Rom. 11:5) are worked out in a masterly fashion by Paul in his letter to the Romans. The messianically restored people of God, the true Israel, is chosen by grace (Rom. 11:6), and because God chooses by grace alone, therefore the call of God is "irrevocable" (Rom. 11:29). "But it is not as though the word of God has failed," he writes (Rom. 9:6), because his Word, his call, creates the messianically reconstituted people of God, the true and new Israel. "For not all who are descended from Israel belong to Israel, and not all are children of Abraham because they are his descendants; but 'Through Isaac shall your descendants be named.' This means that it is not the children of the flesh who are the children of God, but the children of the promise are reckoned as descendants" (Rom. 9:6 – 8). And thus the transition is made from the Israel bound together by blood relationship with Abraham to the Israel bound together by the Spirit in the body of Christ. The same God who called Israel into being has now called the church into being to carry out his purposes in the world.

With this brief historical sketch as a background, let us now look for further illumination of the concept of vocation in the New Testament.

1. *God takes the initiative to call persons through the Holy Spirit into his fellowship to be a holy people, the communion of saints, the body of Christ, the* ekklesia.

God takes the initiative. He moves before people can anticipate their destiny; he acts according to his own purposes; he offers to bestow his gifts out of pure grace. Our Lord himself is reported in the Fourth Gospel as saying to his disciples, "You did not choose me, but I chose you and appointed you" (John 15:16). And the theme is taken up after Pentecost by the leaders of the church. In the letter to the Ephesians a Christian's calling is pushed back to "before the foundation of the world" when God "destined us in love to be his sons through Jesus Christ" (Eph. 1:4 – 5). The emphasis upon the divine initiative is especially strong in a well-known passage in Paul's letter to the Romans.

> We know that in everything God works for good with those who love him, who are called according to his purpose. For those whom he foreknew he also predestined to be conformed to the image of his Son, in order that he might be the first-born among many brethren. And those whom he predestined he also called; and those whom he called he also justified; and those whom he justified he also glorified (Rom. 8:28 – 30; cf. 9:23 – 24, and 2 Thess. 2:13 – 15).

Other New Testament statements make the same claim. In 2 Tim. 1:9 we read: God has "saved us and called us with a holy calling, not in virtue of our works but in virtue of his own purpose and the grace which he gave us in Christ Jesus." Likewise in 2 Pet. 1:3: "His divine power has granted to us all things that pertain to life and godliness, through the knowledge of him who called us to his own glory and excellence, by which he has granted to us his precious and very great promises."

Furthermore, God calls persons not into a "unilateral" relationship with him but into a corporate relationship. Christian vocation *is* corporate. "You are a chosen race, a royal priesthood, a holy nation, God's own people, that you may declare the wonderful deeds of him who called you out of darkness into his marvelous light. Once you were no people but now you are God's people" (1 Pet. 2:9 – 10). People are called into unity with Christ and with each other; they "share in a heavenly call," as the author of Hebrews puts it (Heb. 3:1). The calling is not a private possession. Again we must turn to Paul for a classical statement of this truth.

> For just as the body is one and has many members, and all the members of the body, though many, are one body, so it is with Christ. For by one Spirit we were all baptized into one body—Jews or Greeks, slaves or free—and all were made to drink of one Spirit. For the body does not consist of one member but of many. . . . If one member suffers, all suffer together; if one member is honored, all rejoice together. Now you are the body of Christ and individually members of it (1 Cor. 12:12 – 14, 26 – 27).

2. *The Holy Spirit calls persons to different functions in the body of Christ as God has bestowed upon them his gifts.*

The New Testament records specific instances where persons were called to special tasks within the community of faith. Jesus himself not only called the Twelve "to be with him" (Mark 1:16 – 20; 3:13 – 19) but also sent them out to preach and to heal (Luke 9:1 – 6; cf. Mark 6:7 – 13). Special assignments were also made within the circle of the Twelve. Peter, James, and John constituted an inner circle, and performed certain extraordinary roles, such as accompanying Jesus up to the Mount of Transfiguration (Matt. 17:1 – 8). Peter appears to be the chief spokesman for the Twelve, as for example in the conversation on the way to Caesarea Philippi about the Messiahship of Jesus (Mark 8:27 – 30). Even Judas was given the special task of treasurer of the little group (John 13:29).

Paul frequently refers to his own call to be an apostle: "Paul, a servant of Jesus Christ, called to be an apostle, set apart for the gospel of God" (Rom. 1:1; cf. Gal. 1:15). Within his call to the apostleship Paul was also called to particular places at particular times. Sometimes the call came through the church: "While they were worshiping the Lord and fasting, the Holy Spirit said, 'Set apart for me Barnabas and Saul for the work to which I have called them.' Then after fasting and praying they laid their hands on them and sent them off" (Acts 13:2 – 3). Sometimes the call came directly: "And a vision appeared to Paul in the night: a man of Macedonia was standing beseeching him and saying, 'Come over to Macedonia and help us.' And when he had seen the vision, immediately we sought to go on into Macedonia, concluding that God had called us to preach the gospel to them" (Acts 16:9 – 10). On the basis of his own experience and the experience of the whole Christian community Paul develops what might be called a theology of callings (services) within the church:

> Now there are varieties of gifts, but the same Spirit; and there are varieties of service, but the same Lord; and there are varieties of working, but it is the same God who inspires them all in every one. To each is given the manifestation of the Spirit for the common good. To one is given through the Spirit the utterance of wisdom, and to another the utterance of knowledge according to the same Spirit, to another faith by the same Spirit, to another gifts of healing by the one Spirit, to another the working of miracles, to another prophecy, to another the ability to distinguish between spirits, to another various kinds of tongues, to another the interpretation of tongues. All these

are inspired by one and the same Spirit, who apportions to each one individually as he wills. . . . And God has appointed in the church first apostles, second prophets, third teachers, then workers of miracles, then healers, helpers, administrators, speakers in various kinds of tongues (1 Cor. 12:4–11, 28).

Does the New Testament affirm that God directly calls persons into secular occupations? Let us examine the principal passage, namely, 1 Cor. 7:17–24, which is frequently interpreted to support the view that God calls persons to be engineers in the same way that he called Paul to be an apostle.

> Let every one lead the life which the Lord has assigned to him, and in which God has called him. This is my rule in all the churches. Was any one at the time of his call already circumcised? Let him not seek to remove the marks of circumcision. Was any one at the time of his call uncircumcised? Let him not seek circumcision. For neither circumcision counts for anything nor uncircumcision, but keeping the commandments of God. Every one should remain in the state in which he was called. Were you a slave when called? Never mind. But if you can gain your freedom, avail yourself of the opportunity. For he who was called in the Lord as a slave is a freedman of the Lord. Likewise he who was free when called is a slave of Christ. You were bought with a price; do not become slaves of men. So, brethren, in whatever state each was called, there let him remain with God.

Paul goes on to say, in connection with the question of whether or not to marry, that he is giving this counsel to remain in a present state because "the appointed time has grown very short" (1 Cor. 7:29). Changing status is hardly worth the trouble, since very soon all earthly status will disappear at the Parousia. Remain in your present state if at all possible and serve God there in keeping with his heavenly calling.

The key verses are 17, 20, and 24. They have been variously interpreted. In the Revised Standard Version it is clear that the translators took the position that the calling referred to in the text is the calling of God in Christ to be his own people. This calling comes to people in all stations in life, in all types of situations—slave and free, circumcised and uncircumcised, married and unmarried. Persons who hear the divine calling and respond should remain where they are, and live a life worthy of their calling into a new relationship with God in the church. The translators of the King James Version seem to have taken a different position, namely, that calling means both (a) the calling of God into fellowship and (b) the believer's station in life.

It can be argued that the Revised Standard Version translators have taken some liberty with the text inasmuch as in v. 20 the noun *klesis* is translated "state," while the verb form *kalein* is translated "called." The King James Version translators have, on the other hand, used "calling" and "called," respectively, to translate the two words. Technically, this may be a valid objection, but the King James Version nevertheless does violence to Pauline thought (and, indeed, to New Testament thought) as a whole.

Note should be taken that 1 Cor. 7:20 is the only instance in the entire New Testament where *klesis* seems to indicate station or status in the world. In every other case it is used to describe the action of God in bringing human beings into fellowship with him or in summoning a person for a particular task in the church. It must be said, therefore, that 1 Cor. 7:17 – 24 does not equate calling with occupation, at least in the strict sense. Granting for the moment that *klesis* is used in v. 20, its reference in the context is to marriage, slavery, and circumcision—not to carpentry or weaving! Paul gives no indication that he regarded tentmaking as a calling. His calling was to sainthood and apostleship.

Let it be said, however, that the value and the necessity of secular work are affirmed in the New Testament. Jesus worked as a carpenter before he began his public ministry (Mark 6:3), thus dignifying manual labor. Paul made tents for a living even after he launched upon his ministry (Acts 18:3), so that (a) his motivation for preaching the gospel could not be questioned and (b) he would not be a burden. So he writes to the Thessalonians: "You remember our labor and toil, brethren; we worked night and day, that we might not burden any of you, while we preached to you the gospel of God" (1 Thess. 2:9). Christians should work to provide not only for their own needs but also for those of their brothers and sisters in the faith. "If any one does not provide for his relatives, and especially for his own family, he has disowned the faith and is worse than an unbeliever" (1 Tim. 5:8). Idleness is a sin against God and the community; in fact, "if anyone will not work, let him not eat" (2 Thess. 3:10 – 12). Christians should be "ready for any honest work" (Titus 3:1). And their work should be so done that they "may command the respect of outsiders" (1 Thess. 4:11 – 12).

The primary motivation of the Christian in daily work, however, is not to make a good impression upon those outside the household of faith. Rather, Christians should do their work "not in the way of eyeservice, as men-pleasers, but as servants of Christ" (Eph. 6:5 – 9). For a Christian's whole life, including labor, comes under this injunction: "Whatever you do, in word or deed, do everything in the name of the Lord Jesus" (Col. 3:17; cf. 1 Cor. 10:31).

It is true, however, that the vast majority of statements in the New Testament concerning work unmistakably refer to work in the church or of the church, namely, ministering to the household of believers and bringing others into that household. The much-quoted phrase "fellow workers for God" (1 Cor. 3:9; cf. Rom. 16:9) clearly refers not to secular employment but to the work of making Christ known. And the same is true of Paul's well-known appeal to the Corinthians to stand firm "always abounding in the work of the Lord, knowing that in the Lord your labor is not in vain" (1 Cor. 15:58). That there are valid implications in these passages for all work cannot be denied, and these will be considered at a later point, but here we are concerned only to understand what the Scriptures do or do not say on the subject of vocation.

3. *In Christ, God calls his people to a life of sanctification, whatever their stations may be, in obedience to the Holy Spirit.*

The people of God are "called to be saints together with all those who in every place call on the name of our Lord Jesus Christ, both their Lord and ours" (1 Cor. 1:2). This label "saints," frequently applied in the New Testament to members of the body of Christ, does not, of course, mean that the bearers are free from sin. Saints (or holy ones) are those whom God has separated for a purpose. Thus, the Old Testament can speak of the "holy mountain" not because its rocks are more refined but because God chose it for a particular purpose. A Christian is *simul justus et peccator* ("at the same time justified and a sinner") and remains so until the end of this age. Rather are the saints (*hagioi*) summoned to be "separated" from the world, not in geographical isolation but in their nonconformity to merely secular norms. "Do not be conformed to this world but be transformed by the renewal of your mind, that you may prove what is the will of God, what is good and acceptable and perfect" (Rom. 12:2). A person is a saint by the grace of God, but is expected to grow in grace, "to mature manhood, to the measure of the stature of the fulness of Christ" (Eph. 4:13).

The New Testament is full of exhortations to those who have been called into the body of Christ to be worthy of that calling. *The whole life of the Christian becomes, therefore, part and parcel of vocation under God.* Having been bought with a price, the Christian lays his or her whole being upon the altar in complete dedication to the Creator and Redeemer. "To this end we always pray for you," writes Paul to the Thessalonians, "that our God may make you worthy of his call, and may fulfill every good resolve and work of faith by his power, so that the name of our Lord Jesus may be glorified in you, and you in him" (2 Thess. 1:11 – 12).

A Christian's life is rooted and grounded in the life of the community of believers. First of all, then, vocation has certain implications for a person's relationships with the community. It is essential that in the church the Christian must "lead a life worthy of the calling to which [he has] been called" (Eph. 4:1). In fact, most of the exhortations to live a life consistent with one's calling have as their point of application the household of faith even though many of them are quoted today in preaching and teaching within a much wider context. The original intention must not be forgotten, however, because unless Christians take their calling seriously within the church, there is not much hope of their taking it seriously in the world outside the church.

Although a Christian's life is rooted and grounded in the community of believers, most of his or her life, quantitatively speaking, is lived in the world. Consequently, the vocation of a Christian has certain implications for relationships outside the community. As noted above in the consideration of daily work, a Christian cannot be satisfied to do just as well in the world of work as nonbelievers; but must yet do more and more; the Christian must go the second mile. The New Testament writers try to describe the meaning of this for Christians in various stations in life. The following quotation from 1 Peter (2:18 – 21) is merely illustrative: "Servants, be submissive to your master with all respect, not only to the kind and gentle but also to the overbearing. For one is approved if, mindful of God, he endures pain while suffering unjustly. For what credit is it, if when you do wrong and are beaten for it you take it patiently? But if when you do right and suffer for it you take it patiently, you have God's approval. For to this year you have been called, because Christ also suffered for you, leaving you an example, that you should follow in his steps."

These, in summary, are the meanings of vocation in the New Testament: (a) God calls persons into the church through repentance and faith in Christ; (b) within the church he calls certain individuals to perform special functions; and (c) he calls all members of the body of Christ to a holy life in all their relationships. The similarity of these meanings to the meanings of vocation discovered in the Old Testament is obvious, and the similarity is not accidental.

Because God chose Israel to be his people, and delivered them out of bondage, he expected the Israelites to behave toward him, toward each other, and toward the world in a very special way, spelled out in terms of the law and sealed by a covenant. In like manner God has delivered us from bondage through Christ the Liberator, called us to be the New Israel, and expects us to behave toward him, toward each other, and toward the world in a very special way, spelled out in terms of faith active in love and sealed by the blood of a new covenant.

An overarching theme of both Testaments is the calling of the people of God—not "the flight of the alone to the Alone." This contrast draws attention to two distinctions: First, God, not humankind, takes the initiative. Second, persons in community, not individuals in isolation, is the divine goal. Vocation is basically corporate, but in a derivative sense it is also individual. There is only one calling of God, and this calling lays claim to a person's whole life both in the community of faith and in the world. This is vocation according to the Scriptures.

3

LUTHER'S UNDERSTANDING OF VOCATION

The New Testament recognizes only one calling of God—a calling that redeems life in the body of Christ and that lays claim to life, to a person's whole life, both in the community of faith and in the world. And so Paul writes to all the members of the church at Thessalonica: "We always pray for you, that our God may make you worthy of his call, and may fulfill every good resolve and work of faith by his power, so that the name of our Lord Jesus may be glorified in you" (2 Thess. 1:11 – 12). Every Christian has a vocation!

Furthermore, in the New Testament the Christian life is portrayed as being in the world although not of it. There is no indication that Christians should withdraw from participation in the established social order, either by geographical segregation or by denying certain basic human functions and relationships.

Another point of view had appeared by the beginning of the fourth century. Eusebius, for example, writes about A.D. 315 as follows:

> *Two* ways of life were thus given by the law of Christ to His Church. The *one* is above nature, and beyond common human living; it admits not marriage, child-bearing, property nor the possession of wealth, but wholly and permanently separate from the common customary life of mankind, it devotes itself to the service of God alone in its wealth of heavenly love! . . . Such then is the perfect form of the Christian life. And the *other*, more humble, more human, permits men to join in pure nuptials and to produce children, to undertake government, to give orders to soldiers fighting for right; it allows them to have minds for farming, for trade, and the other more secular interests as well as for religion; and it is for them that times of retreat and instruction, and days for hearing sacred things are set apart. *And a kind of secondary grade of piety it attributed to them.* (Italics mine)[1]

One can find no explicit reference to vocation; but now there are two classes of Christians—those who live "above nature" and those who remain in nature, living a "more human" life. This distinction having been made, there followed a rapid growth of monasticism and of the belief that only celibate withdrawal from human society had the full approval of God.

Where Luther Differed from Rome

By the fifteenth century the division between ordinary Christians and Christians seeking perfection had become complete. It meant a fatal recognition of a double standard of conduct and of responsibility: one for the monk, the nun, and the priest and the other for the believer who continued his or her activities in the everyday world. And the term "vocation" was applied only to the former. *Only the monk, the nun, and the priest had callings.* Christians in the secular world had no vocations.

So it was that monasteries and convents played a central role in the life of the medieval church. Monks and nuns by separating themselves from the world gained positive merit both for themselves and for those who remained in the world. Life was a two-story affair, with farmers, soldiers, and artisans on the ground level keeping the wheels of normal human life going and with those committed to obedience, poverty, and celibacy on the second level with their eyes (supposedly) fixed upon heaven.

Against this stratification of Christendom, this sharp distinction between the secular and the sacred, Luther rebelled. A human being is not justified before God by what he or she does or does not do in relation to other persons. Perfection is demanded of all people—not just of those in the cloister. And human beings, regardless of where they live, are all incapable of perfection. Monks are no better than masons in the sight of the High and Holy One. The salvation of both monks and masons depends entirely upon the unmerited grace of God shed abroad in Christ, the Savior.

Out of gratitude and love, insisted Luther, Christians will gladly serve others in whatever situation they find themselves, and with absolutely no expectation of reward either from God or humanity. Only a person liberated by Christ can afford to live like that. And such a person can afford it because in Christ he or she has everything needed for time and eternity. Persons liberated by Christ can forget about merit and can concentrate upon others' needs.

Having rejected the basis for the medieval double standard of Christian living, Luther had two alternatives before him in regard to vocation: (a) he could proceed to deny the validity of vocation with reference to any station in life; or (b) he could extend vocation to include all stations in life, clerical and lay, "spiritual" and "secular." He chose the second alternative and thereby ushered in a new era of understanding of and concern for Christian vocation in the Western world.

Luther's concept of vocation, like a coin, has two sides—but it is one coin. On one side he conceives of vocation as gospel, as a call to life in Christ and in his body, the church; on the other side he conceives of vocation as law, as a call to obedience and service.

One cannot understand Luther's concept of vocation without reference to his even more basic concept of the two kingdoms (realms): the kingdom of grace and the kingdom of creation. Both are God's kingdoms. Yet they must never be merged, and *never be separated*. Furthermore, they are coordinate realms: one cannot be subordinated to the other. The kingdom of grace is on the right hand; the kingdom of creation is on the left hand. The kingdom of grace is the realm of faith and of the freedom of the children of God. The kingdom of creation is the realm where the believer serves God by serving others. In this realm persons may cooperate with God, in faith, in the achievement of his purposes. God may also use persons as his instruments even though they may not be aware of the roles they are playing.

It is important and illuminating to note that Luther's concept of vocation is applicable to both kingdoms: God calls persons into the kingdom of grace, where he bestows upon them forgiveness and fellowship, and he calls persons to serve their fellows in the kingdom of creation. Just as both kingdoms belong to the one God, so do both the life of unmerited grace and the life of obedient service belong to one vocation.

Vocation as Grace

God calls persons through the Holy Spirit to a life of divine forgiveness and fellowship in the church. This primary understanding is clearly evident in Luther's explanation of the Third Article of the Creed in his Small Catechism.

> I believe that by my own reasons or strength I cannot believe in Jesus Christ, my Lord, or come to him. But the *Holy Spirit has called (berufen) me through the Gospel,* enlightened me with his gifts, and sanctified and preserved

me in true faith, *just as he calls (beruft), gathers, enlightens, and sanctifies the whole Christian church* on earth and preserves it in union with Jesus Christ in the one true faith. In this Christian church he daily and abundantly forgives all my sins, and the sins of all believers, and on the last day he will raise me and all the dead and will grant eternal life to me and to all who believe in Christ. This is most certainly true. *(Italics mine)*[2]

The reference to the calling of the church receives further support and elucidation in the Large Catechism, as follows:

> I believe that there is on earth a little holy flock or *community of pure saints* under one head, Christ. It is *called together (zusammen-berufen) by the Holy Spirit* in one faith, mind, and understanding. It possesses a variety of gifts, yet is united in love without sect or schism. Of this community I also am a part and member, a participant and co-partner in all the blessings it possesses. (Italics mine)[3]

It is difficult to determine from these quotations whether Luther regarded the call in this primary sense as being basically individual or basically corporate. Within the whole context of Luther's writings we are warranted in affirming that Luther emphasized the divine call to the individual, but at the same time he recognized that there is no call apart from the church. Even as the calling together of the whole church goes on to the end of time, so the calling of individuals into the church goes on to the end of time. It is the same calling, looked at from different perspectives. As the Holy Spirit calls, enlightens, and sanctifies the church, so he calls, enlightens, and sanctifies each and every believer.

Unless God called, there would be no faith in Jesus Christ, there would be no church. Human beings cannot by their own reason or strength believe in Jesus Christ or come to him. God must and does take the initiative to bring faith into being, to bring the church into being. Limited by finitude and sinfulness, human beings are otherwise doomed to a pitifully cramped and frustrating existence. They never know how cramped and frustrating it is, however, until God draws near and calls them into an entirely different kind of existence. The divine call is, therefore, a divine gift, a manifestation of grace, the gospel extended to hapless persons in the place where they are.

This, then, is the primary meaning of calling as understood by Luther. Without this understanding clearly established, misunderstanding of everything else he said on the subject is almost certain to follow.

Vocation as Service

God continues to call those who embrace his offer of forgiveness and fellowship to a life of loving service in all their relationships. This understanding of vocation is a derivative, a corollary of the primary meaning.

It must be recognized that vocation as service bulks larger in Luther's writings than vocation as fellowship in the church. This weighting in favor of the derivative rather than the primary meaning of calling must be seen in the light of two considerations.

In the first place, it must be remembered that Luther's most frequent use of the term "vocation" was in polemical reaction to the use of the term in the Roman Church. In rejecting completely Rome's restrictive use of the term, it was necessary for Luther to emphasize (even overemphasize) his new, evangelical understanding of vocation as being applicable to every believer.

Second, Luther used many other concepts and metaphors to depict the seeking, searching, probing activity of God in relation to his fallen creatures. For example, in a sermon for the First Sunday in Advent he interprets our Lord's entry into Jerusalem as signifying God's initiative toward the human soul. "This is what is meant by 'Thy King Cometh.' You do not seek him, but he seeks you. You do not find him, he finds you. For the preachers come from him, not from you; their sermons come from him, not from you; your faith comes from him, not from you; everything that faith works in you comes from him, not from you; and where he does not come, you remain outside."[4]

A word must be said about Luther's use of 1 Cor. 7:17 – 24, especially v. 20: "Every one should remain in the state *(klesei)* in which he was called *(eklethe)*." Luther translates *klesei* as *Ruf* and *elkethe* as *berufen ist*. He usually uses *Stand* to signify station. Nevertheless, for all practical purposes Luther uses vocation *(Beruf)* to cover both calling into the church and calling in a station, with emphasis upon the second usage. Gustaf Wingren seems to be correct when he says that "Luther does not use *Beruf* or *vocatio* in reference to the work of a non-Christian. All have station *(Stand)* and office *(Amt* or *Stelle)*; but *Beruf* is the Christian's earthly or spiritual work."[5] The reason this distinction is not always maintained by Luther is that he was writing about and for Christians, who had both *Stand* and *Beruf*.

Let us now examine more closely Luther's understanding of vocation as loving service.

1. *Every Christian has a vocation in life because every believer has a station, and in every station there are opportunities for service.* Vocation includes the total life of a person—not simply his or her occupation. God calls persons to lay their whole lives on the altar of dedication. Vocation involves all relationships.

A Christian is called to be a faithful spouse; to be a wise and understanding parent; to be a responsible citizen; to be a good neighbor; just as the Christian is called to be a competent carpenter. In fact, it is not necessary to have a job in the popular sense in order to have a vocation. A retired carpenter, stricken by illness and lying helpless in bed, still has a vocation from the Lord.

All this Luther makes quite clear in his sermon on the Gospel lesson for the day of St. John the Evangelist (John 21:19 – 24). On the basis of this passage he addressed some illuminating admonitions to those who feel they have no vocation.

> You may reply: But how if I am not called? Answer: How is it possible that you are not called? You have always been in some state or station; you have always been a husband or wife, a boy or girl, or servant. Picture before you the humblest state. Are you a husband, and you think you have not enough to do in that sphere to govern your wife, children, domestics, and property so that all may be obedient to God and you do no one any wrong? . . . Again: Are you a son or daughter, and do you think you have not enough work with yourself, to continue chaste, pure, and temperate during your youth, obey your parents, and offend no one by word or deed? . . . Again: Are you a domestic servant, and do you think you would go idle if you were to serve your lord or mistress with all faithfulness as your station and orders require, and also keep your mouth under control as with a bridle? . . . And again: Are you a prince, a lord, spiritual or secular—who has more to do than you, in order that your subjects may do right, preserve peace, and wrong is done by no one? . . . See, as no one is without some commission and calling, so no one is without some kind of work, if he desires to do what is right. Every one, therefore, is to take heed to continue in his calling, look to himself, faithfully do what is commanded him, and serve God and keep his commandments; then he will have so much to do that all time will be too short, all places too cramped, all resources of help too weak.[6]

Note the wide sweep of vocation in Luther's thought. Everything is included from a husband's governing his household, to a daughter's keeping herself chaste, to a servant's holding his tongue, to a prince ruling his realm. Note, furthermore, that Luther thinks of all these activities as in some sense "work," i.e., that which God expects of a person. Therefore, Luther says: "If you are a student, mind your studies; if you are a maid, sweep the house; if you are a servant, care for the horses; etc."[7]—and in so doing you will be fulfilling your vocation in the world.

2. *Vocation is given structure by God through "orders" and "offices" which, because divinely decreed, serve good and necessary purposes even though some of them may involve evil persons and seemingly evil actions.* The affirmation of divinely decreed orders and offices imparts a realism to Luther's understanding of vocation in the world and at the same time safeguards a Christian's conscience.

The three primary orders that God the Creator has provided are the family, the state, and the organized church, and every Christian belongs to all three orders. Luther identified, rather naively, the economic order with that of the family. These orders will stand until the end of the world. They are a part of the basic structure of human existence. Within these orders there are offices, which may change from time to time, but while they are operative, God works through them.

When faithful and dedicated persons hold offices that enjoy God's blessing, the requirements of these offices become the responsibility of God himself. For example, within the order of the state are many offices which require that the officeholders do things that Christians, motivated by love, are hesitant to do. There are "the offices of the sword" (especially the judge, the executioner, the soldier), which involve condemning people to death, executing criminals, or slaying human beings in battle. In regard to these offices Luther writes:

> The sword is in itself right and is a divine and useful ordinance, which God will not have despised, but feared, honored, and obeyed, on pain of vengeance, as Paul says, in Romans xiii. For He has established two kinds of government among men. The one is spiritual; it has no sword. . . . The other is worldly government, through the sword, which aims to keep peace among men.[8]

Therefore, Christians who must use the sword in the fulfillment of their official duties can do so with a free conscience, according to Luther.

This does not mean that all actions of an officeholder are ipso facto the actions of God and consequently defensible actions. It must not be forgotten that all officeholders are sinners and can pervert their true responsibilities. So Luther makes a careful distinction "between an occupation and the man who is in it, between a work and the doer of it. An occupation can be good and right in itself and yet bad and wrong if the man in the occupation . . . does not do his duty rightly."[9] In fact, "where is there an office or a work or any other thing so good that self-willed, wicked people do not abuse it?"[10]

Closely related to Luther's concept of orders and offices is that of the divine masks or *larvae*, through which God reveals himself. The Most High never reveals himself to people in his naked transcendence. Christ in his incarnation was a mask of God, and through this mask God made himself known, acted on humanity's behalf. A mask both conceals and reveals the Creator. So it is that orders and offices and stations are also *larvae Dei* through which God is constantly confronting human beings with his will and power.

Still another concept of Luther is that of a person being a conduit or channel through which the love and power of God may flow. All good things come from above, and a person in his or her vocation is merely an instrument through which the divine activity takes place. It is essential that human beings keep themselves "open" as channels through which the divine love and power may flow, and this is accomplished by God himself in Word and Sacrament, in forgiveness and fellowship.

3. *Everything a Christian does in his or her vocation is for the sake of others, for the sake of their spiritual, physical, moral, or cultural welfare.* In the broadest sense, Christians are called to work for the common welfare, but they do this in very specific ways within the context of their own station in life. "A cobbler, a smith, a farmer, . . . by means of his own work or office must benefit and serve every other, that in this way many kinds of work may be done for the bodily and spiritual welfare of the community, even as all the members of the body serve one another."[11]

A corollary of this thesis is that nothing a person does in his or her vocation has any relevance to eternal salvation. Being a faithful spouse, a wise and understanding parent, a responsible citizen, a good neighbor, and a competent carpenter will not win a Christian any "extra points" in the celestial record book. A Christian's status in the kingdom of heaven is secured by grace alone. In Luther's own words, "Christ has done and accomplished everything for you, atoned for your sins, secured grace and life and salvation."[12]

Still another corollary is that a person in his or her vocation "need not do any work for God nor for the departed saints." With reference to God, the person is complete and needs absolutely nothing; and with reference to "the departed saints," it is too late to do anything for them. God can use a Christian to bring his blessings to human beings, but he does not himself need a Christian. And so Luther delivers a blunt warning: "If you find a work by which you benefit God or his saints or yourself and not your neighbor, know that such a work is *not* good." "Hence direct all the good you can do and your whole life to the end that it may be good; but it is good only when it is useful to other people."[13]

A Christian's vocation of service should not be one of grim duty, of sternly accepted obligation. Luther never ceases to remind his readers that service should flow freely, spontaneously from love, which is in turn the gift of God. He does this most beautifully, of course, in his "Treatise on Christian Liberty," in which he writes as follows: "Lo, this is a truly Christian life, here faith is truly effectual through love; that is, it issues in works of the freest service cheerfully and lovingly done, with which a man willingly serves another without hope of reward, and for himself is satisfied with the fulness and wealth of his faith."[14] Luther's strong conviction that true service is always filled with joy is well summarized by Wingren:

> Love does not think about doing works, it finds joy in people; and when something good is done for others, that does not appear to love as works but simply as gifts which flow naturally from love. . . . He who has the Holy Spirit knows it by the fact, among others, that in faith and gladness he fulfils his vocation. . . . Finding love is thus the same thing as finding both neighbor and vocation to be something in which one can live with joy.[15]

And what is the final test of the validity of a person's vocation in the world? Just this: "Christ at the last day will not ask how much you have prayed, fasted, pilgrimaged, done this or that for yourself, but how much good you have done to others, even the very least."[16]

4. *All service in vocation ranks the same with God, and Christians may with equal confidence hold the lowest and the highest offices, but certain offices in themselves are of greater significance than others.* Inasmuch as a person can achieve no merit with God by virtue of service in vocation, no office from the divine perspective can have an advantage over another. So long as an office serves the common welfare, it is pleasing in God's sight and should be held in honor as the work of God.

There are differences between offices, however, that cannot be denied.

The qualifications demanded by various offices differ greatly, both in native ability and in training. These differences in turn result in distinctions in social status and financial compensation. Such distinctions will always exist in any society. More important are the differences in significance for the common welfare. Obviously, a ditchdigger makes a contribution of far less significance to the common welfare than does a physician or a mayor of a city. Making a scale of offices on the basis of their relative value to a community necessarily involves a good deal of subjectivity. It is interesting and illuminating to note how Luther rates some of the occupations of his day.

At the top of the list he places the office of pastor. "There is no dearer treasure, nor any more precious thing on earth or in this life than a real and faithful pastor or preacher."[17] This statement, it should be noted, does not make the office of pastor superior to all others, but it does deny that there is another office of greater significance. At other places, however, he does give the pastoral office an edge over all others, and that for two reasons: (a) other offices were "not purchased at so dear a price as the preaching office, with the blood and the death of the Son of God"; and (b) the pastoral office deals with matters of eternal consequence, whereas all other offices are concerned with "this temporal, transient life."[18] Nevertheless, he feels that the pastoral office does not require as great native gifts as do other offices, notably that of law.[19] Also, by exalting the pastoral office he does not intend to imply that "every man must train his child for this office, for not all the boys must become pastors."[20]

Next on the list Luther places teaching. He even admits that sometimes he cannot make up his mind whether preaching or teaching is the higher office. "I myself," he writes, "if I could leave the preaching office and other things, or had to do so, would not be so glad to have any other work as that of schoolmaster, or teacher of boys, for I know that this is the most useful, the greatest, and the best, next to the work of preaching. Indeed, I scarcely know which of the two is the better." Of one thing he is certain, namely, that "a diligent and pious schoolteacher or master, or whoever it is that faithfully trains and teaches boys, can never be sufficiently rewarded, or repaid with any money."[21]

For third place Luther names "the office of worldly government," which he describes as "a glorious ordinance of God and splendid gift of God."[22] "It is a necessary office and rank, which we can no more do without than we can do without life itself, since without government this life cannot continue."[23] To those in the office of worldly government Luther pays this extraordinary tribute:

> Just as a pious theologian and sincere preacher is called, in the realm of Christ, an angel of God, a savior, prophet, priest, servant, and teacher, so a pious jurist and true scholar can be called, in the worldly realm of the emperor, a prophet, priest, angel, and savior. . . . When I speak of the jurists, I do not mean only the Doctors of Laws, but the whole profession, including chancellors, secretaries, judges, advocates, notaries, and all who have to do with the legal side of government.[24]

Somewhat below the offices of pastor, teacher, and lawyer Luther places other offices for which he has a high regard, namely, those of physician, writer, secretary, and "scholars in the liberal arts." His list, of course, is not meant to be exhaustive.

5. *A Christian should rejoice in having a vocation in the world and should remain in his or her station rather than try to escape it.* As we have seen, in Luther's judgment the vast majority of stations in life are ordained of God, and pleasing to him. All such stations are not equally pleasant, but they can all bring blessings to the believer's neighbors. To rebel against one's station in the world is a serious matter.

In his exposition of Psalm 111, Luther applies the first part of v. 3, "Full of honor and adornment is his work," to the stations of men:

> This is a thanksgiving for all the works of God which he ordains among men, as, for example, the various situations, offices, and duties among men. Surely, anyone should laugh in his heart for joy if he finds himself in a station that God instituted or ordained. He ought to shout and dance as he thanks God for such a divine act, because here he hears and is assured that his position is full of honor and adornment before God. . . . Now, this means that a servant, maid, son, daughter, man, woman, lord, subject, or whoever else may belong to a station ordained by God, as long as he fills his station, is as beautiful and glorious in the sight of God as a bride adorned for her marriage or as the image of a saint decorated for a high festival.[25]

It is incomprehensible to Luther why "the blind and senseless world will not see this." On the contrary, the world "despises such stations so shamefully," complains Luther, "that it makes a pious heart bleed."[26]

Consequently, because of this prevalent attitude, people are always trying to escape their stations. "Is one married, then he praises the state of one who has no wife; has he none, then he praises the married state. Is he in a spiritual calling, then he likes the secular; is he in a secular calling, then he prefers the spiritual."[27] When a person will not accept his station, so that it comes within his vocation, there is little that God can do with him. "It is much to be lamented," says Luther in his *Table Talk*, "that no man is content and satisfied with that which God gives him in his vocation. . . . To serve God is for every one to remain in his vocation, . . . be it ever so mean and simple."[28]

Only if a person's station is inherently sinful should it be abandoned. What does Luther mean by a station that is sinful in itself? Here is his answer:

> When I speak of a calling which in itself is not sinful, I do not mean that we can live on the earth without sin. All callings and estates sin daily; but I mean the calling God has instituted is not opposed to God, as for example, marriage, man-servant, maid-servant, lord, wife, superintendent, ruler, judge, officer, farmer, citizen, etc. I mention as sinful stations in life: robbery, usury, public women, and, as they are at present, the pope, cardinals, bishops, priests, monks and nuns, who neither preach nor listen to preaching.[29]

To be in an "irksome" station is one thing; to be in a sinful station is quite another thing. Blessed is one who can distinguish between the two, and acts accordingly.

6. *Inasmuch as all offices should be open to all qualified persons, education should be encouraged to the end that students may be adequately prepared for appropriate offices.* The one exception Luther made to this sweeping statement are the offices held by nobility and therefore filled on a hereditary basis.

His strong conviction that all offices should be open to properly qualified young persons considerably softens the hardness of his conviction that persons should remain in the stations where God has placed them. Here is the chief passage which cracks the rigidity of the medieval pattern of stations:

> We ought to know that God is a wonderful lord. His trade is to take beggars and make them lords, even as He makes all things out of nothing. This trade of His no one will interfere with or hinder. He has the whole world sing of Him, in Psalm cxii, "Who is like the Lord, Who sitteth so high and beholdeth so deep? Who lifteth the small out of the dust and raiseth the poor out of the filth, that He may make them sit among the princes, even among the princes of His people." Look about you, at the courts of all the kings and princes, at the cities and the parishes; see whether this Psalm does not rule

with many strong examples. There you will find jurists, doctors, counsellors, writers, preachers, who were usually poor and have certainly been boys at school, and have mounted and flown up by their pens (feathers), until they are lords, as the Psalm says, and like princes, help to rule lands and peoples. It is not God's will that born kings, princes, lords, and nobles should rule and be lords alone; He wills to have His beggars with them, so that they may not think that noble birth alone, and not God alone, makes lords and rulers.[30]

Therefore Luther pleads that young persons be educated for the offices for which they have the proper talents. To parents he says: "If God has given you a child who has the ability and the talent for this office, i.e., pastor, and you do not train him for it, but look only to the belly and to temporal livelihood, see what a pious prig and small potato you are."[31] To the state he says: "I hold that it is the duty of the government to compel its subjects to keep their children in school, especially those children [with special abilities]. . . . Let the government, when it sees a promising boy, have him kept in school; if the father is poor, let it help him."[32] To the wealthy he says: "Let the rich make their wills with this work in view, as some have done who have endowed stipends; that is the right way to bequeath your money to the church. This way you do not, to be sure, release departed souls from purgatory, but by maintaining God's offices, you help the living and those to come who are not yet born."[33]

It must be remembered that in making this plea Luther was thinking of offices as being open to all people, Christians and non-Christians presumably. For a Christian young person his or her office would be one segment of total vocation under God.

It is time to pull together the strands of Luther's understanding of vocation. According to his understanding, God calls persons through the Holy Spirit (a) to a life of divine forgiveness and fellowship in the church and (b) to a life of loving service in all human relationships. Luther focused attention upon vocation as loving service, and therefore as applicable to all Christians, because he was combating the current Roman view that only monks, nuns, and priests had vocations.

In developing the concept of a Christian's vocation of service in the world, Luther affirmed six basic theses: (a) Every Christian has a vocation in the world, because every Christian has a station in which he or she can serve others. (b) Vocation in the world is given structure by means of divinely established orders and offices. (c) Everything a Christian does in his or her vocation in the world is for the sake of human welfare. (d) All service in vocation ranks the same with God, but not all offices have the same significance in society. (e) A Christian should be grateful to have a God-given vocation where he or she can remain in loving service. (f) All young persons should have the opportunity to prepare for the offices for which they are best qualified.

Where Luther Differed from Calvin

What are the similarities between Luther's concept of vocation and Calvin's concept of vocation? In the first place, Luther and Calvin would agree that a Christian's vocation in the world includes far more than an occupation, what is done for pay. Second, Luther and Calvin would agree that all stations in life, even the "mean and simple," enjoy the divine approbation. In the third place, Luther and Calvin would agree that persons may not lightly desert their stations but should willingly serve at their posts without complaint.

On the other hand, there are differences between Luther and Calvin, and these may be largely differences in emphasis. For Luther the primary reason why God gives a Christian a vocation in the world is to encourage a life of loving service, whereas for Calvin the reason seems to be the proper ordering of human life, lest everything be thrown into confusion. It follows that in Calvin's understanding of vocation activity ought to be carefully calculated with a view to its propriety and effectiveness, whereas in Luther's understanding there is much room for spontaneity born of the dynamic of love which has its source in God. Consequently, in Calvin's view vocation affords great consolation, whereas in Luther's view the divine blessing includes both consolation and unbounded joy. Finally, while Calvin sees vocation as a means of giving glory to God, Luther sees it primarily as a means whereby God can bestow his good gifts upon humankind.

Some of the differences from Luther's concept of vocation which were implicit in Calvin's teachings became explicit in the Reformed tradition which developed after Calvin, especially at two points.

1. *In the Reformed tradition vocation is very closely related to predestination.* Vocation provides an excellent opportunity for a person to win assurance that he is among the elect, since God will certainly prosper the undertakings of those whom he has marked as his very own. In other words, confirm your election through your vocation! This view gains support from a passage in 2 Peter (1:3 – 11):

His divine power has granted to us all things that pertain to life and godliness, through the knowledge of him who called us to his own glory and excellence. . . . For this very reason make every effort to *supplement your faith* with virtue, and virtue with knowledge, and knowledge with self-control, and self-control with steadfastness, and steadfastness with godliness, and godliness with brotherly affection, and brotherly affection with love. . . . *Therefore, brethren, be the more zealous to confirm your call and election,* for if you do this you will never fall; so there will be richly provided for you an entrance into the eternal kingdom of our Lord and Savior Jesus Christ. (Italics mine)

It should be noted that believers are exhorted "to supplement" their faith and that "entrance into the eternal kingdom" seems to be contingent upon the supplement! Calvinists made the most of this passage.

It is difficult to reconcile this interpretation of salvation and vocation with that of Luther. According to Luther, a person in vocation in the world can do nothing to secure salvation, which is freely provided in Christ. In a secular vocation a Christian's entire attention is directed to the neighbor and the neighbor's welfare. Assurance of salvation (election) is sufficiently given in Word and Sacrament.

2. *In the Reformed tradition vocation is a call to action, including what we now designate as "social action"*—the translation of the divine righteousness into the structures of human society. In contrast, Luther, on the whole, conceives of vocation in the world within the conventional limits of time-honored social patterns. As a result, the Lutheran interpretation of vocation tended to be quietistic, while the Calvinist interpretation tended in the activist direction. What this meant for the Puritans is forcefully expressed by R. H. Tawney.

On the lips of the Puritan divines, [vocation] is not an invitation to resignation, but the bugle call which summons the elect to the long battle which will end only after death. "The world is all before them." They are to hammer out their salvation, not merely *in vocatione,* but *per vocationem.* The calling is not a condition in which an individual is born, but a strenuous and exacting enterprise, to be undertaken, indeed, under the guidance of Providence, but to be chosen by each man himself, with a deep sense of his solemn responsibilities.[34]

The fact that Luther was deeply suspicious of and bitterly opposed to the rising commercialism of his day, while Calvin recognized the burgeoning world of commerce as an area of legitimate activity for a Christian, had much to do with the direction that vocation took in Reformed Protestantism. Max Weber's thesis[35] that the Calvinist view of vocation provided the inner motivation for the rise of capitalism has been severely criticized, but the fact remains that this view of vocation, as developed in Puritanism, provided a very convenient rationale for the leaders of the capitalistic enterprise.

In trying to grasp Luther's view of work as an expression of vocation we need to keep in mind (a) when he came on the stage of history and (b) what happened after he left the stage. George Forell helps us to remember both points, at the cost of some oversimplification, by affirming that Rome took the position that "work is an evil, at best a necessary evil," while Geneva took the position that "work is the activity which gives life meaning and zest—it is our purpose in life." According to Rome we work in order to live, but according to Geneva we live in order to work. Luther stands somewhere between these two positions. The solution to the problem of work is not to depreciate it and escape it, if possible, as Roman Catholicism advised; nor is the solution the glorification of work itself as in some way the bearer of salvation, as the Neo-Calvinists seemed to imply. "As Luther saw it, God confronts man *in* his daily work and calls him to responsible discipleship right here."[36]

But Luther himself did not have the whole answer. Some weaknesses in his understanding of vocation have already been implied. In the first place, we must never forget that Luther lived in a predominantly feudal society and that much of his thought is shaped accordingly. This also explains to a very large extent his social conservatism, his fear of change and his horror of revolution. Second, he offers little help to a person struggling with "the choice of a lifework." His consideration of vocation usually proceeded on the assumption that human beings were already in their life situations or stations. The problem was not how to find "a lifework" but what to do with one's present station. In his writings on education, however, he did urge parents and princes to see to it that young persons of outstanding aptitudes for particular offices would receive the requisite education. In the third place, Luther's eschatology prevented him from taking a long-range view of vocation. Like Paul, he had a "foreshortened" view of history. Since he expected the imminent end of the world, he apparently saw no point in working out for either church or culture the far-reaching implications of his concept of vocation.

In addition to admitting these "weaknesses," we need to express what can be termed "a regret." As noted at the outset, Luther clearly affirmed in his Small Catechism and in his Large Catechism the primary biblical meaning of vocation, namely, the calling, gathering, enlightening, and sanctifying of the people of God, the church. It is to be regretted that Luther was forced by historical circumstances to give almost his entire attention to the derivative meaning of vocation, namely, the Christian's life of service, to the neglect of the primary meaning. To have done what he did was, of course, an integral and essential aspect of Luther's own calling. Vocation had to be liberated from the narrow limits imposed by Rome. On the other hand, Luther achieved this liberation at the price of failing to develop fully his doctrine of the church and of placing a severe strain upon the biblical view of vocation.

That his concept of vocation had far-reaching implications no historian has ever denied. After Luther, everyday life was never quite the same again. Partly because he did not bother to work out the implications, and partly because of the deep sinfulness of human nature (which he well knew!), his concept of the vocation of the Christian never realized its potential. In fact, the perversions of his concept of vocation during the centuries following Luther down to the present day have been terrible to behold. Nevertheless, what Luther *did* accomplish is succinctly summarized in the words of W. R. Forrester: "Luther, in deposing the monk from his former position as the ideal of a Christian man, and putting the good householder in his place, changed the whole emphasis of Christian ethics, and gave a new start to the history of Europe."[37] In other words, Luther broke the Roman chains which bound vocation and extended the calling of God to include the totality of every Christian's life.

4
THE CALLING OF EVERYMAN TODAY

Having explored the meaning of vocation in the Scriptures and in the writings of Martin Luther, we shall now attempt an answer to the question, What is the calling of Everyman today? The insights gained so far will be utilized in outlining an approach to vocation relevant to our contemporary situation. "Everyman" is taken to mean a representative human being, male or female, in the sense of the famous fifteenth-century morality play with that title.

As soon as one mentions "calling" or "vocation" three basic questions come to mind: Who is calling? To whom is the call addressed? For what purpose is the call? These are very simple questions, questions that are implicit or explicit in all kinds of circumstances where a call is heard.

For six years we lived on a certain block of Claremont Avenue in New York City, just across from Columbia University. On the one side of the street stood Barnard College buildings and on the other side of the street stood apartment buildings which housed families of Columbia faculty and staff. Since the street was a dead end, both the street itself and the wide sidewalks became, after school and over weekends, a veritable playground. At those times, above the noise of children at play down below, one could hear, intermittently, a call from the apartments above: "Johnny! Susie!" Who was calling? A mother. To whom was she calling? Her children. For what purpose did she call? To bring them home—for dinner perhaps, or to run an errand.

Vocation, understood from the perspective of Christian faith, is as simple as that. Who is calling? God. To whom is the call addressed? His children. For what purpose does he call? That his children may come home, to gather around his Table and then to run errands for him. Let us examine these questions and answers.

The Three Basic Questions

Who is calling? To reply that God is calling may appear to be an obvious answer, at least for Christians, but let us not proceed to the next question too quickly. Consider: In the widespread and casual use of the word "vocation" or "calling," to how many persons does the question of *who* is calling ever occur?

Pick up the latest and most highly recommended books on vocational guidance that you may see on the library shelves of a school of education or in the office of a high school counselor and try to find the word "God" in an index. No, you will not find God there, because in the professional field that specializes in helping persons "discover" their "vocations" God has long since been banished. And so we have the weird phenomenon today of callings without a caller—no less weird than the smile of the Cheshire cat without the Cheshire cat in *Alice in Wonderland.* Small wonder that a novelist who is a thoroughgoing naturalist can refer without any sense of incongruity to writing as his "calling."

And so the question of who is calling must be raised and answered. It must be raised by Christians on every occasion when the words "calling" and "vocation" are used in a clearly naturalistic sense. By so doing in a sort of Socratic way, some persons may be sufficiently annoyed, disturbed, even shocked, that they will stop prostituting one of the most significant words in the English language or begin for the first time to wrestle with the fundamental issues of human life and destiny.

But there is another reason for raising the question, namely, to spell out the answer. "God" is indeed the answer, and yet, for the Christian, that is not an adequate answer. Such an answer can be given too glibly. Furthermore, such a minimal answer may actually turn out to be non-Christian, since the concept of God can be given many a different content.

For Christians the One who calls is none other than "God the Father of our Lord Jesus Christ," and this is saying something quite other than "God the unmoved First Mover" and something far more than "the God of Israel." Yes, the answer must be spelled out so that there may be no misunderstanding. Indeed, the answer has been spelled out for us. Why should we struggle with words and phrases when the answer is at hand in the liturgy of the church? He who calls is "the Father, the Almighty, maker of heaven and earth, of all that is, seen and unseen . . . the only Son of God, eternally begotten of the Father. . . . For us and for our salvation he came down from heaven . . . and was made man. . . . The Holy Spirit, the Lord, the giver of life, who proceeds from the Father and the Son. With the Father and the Son he is worshiped and glorified."

To whom is the call addressed? The call of God is addressed to his children, to all his children, everywhere.

This answer immediately poses the problem of *who* are God's children. According to one view, all human beings are children of God by virtue of being the creatures of God. This view is reflected in the popular concept of "the Fatherhood of God and the brotherhood of man," the acceptance of which is supposed to dissolve all difficulties between individuals and between nations! Those taking this position claim the support of the creation story, which affirms that human beings were made in God's image (Gen. 1:26 – 30), and Paul's speech on the Areopagus, to wit:

> And [God] made from one every nation of men to live on all the face of the earth, having determined allotted periods and the boundaries of their habitation, that they should seek God, in the hope that they might feel after him and find him. Yet he is not far from each one of us, for
> "In him we live and move and have our being";
> as even some of your poets have said,
> "For we are indeed his offspring." (Acts 17:26 – 28)

According to the alternative view, both Old and New Testaments have been written in the conviction that human beings are not children by birth (by creation) but become children of God by adoption. Many passages can be quoted to support this position, as, for example, John 1:12 – 13: "To all who received him, who believed in his name, he gave power to become children of God; who were born, not of blood nor of the will of the flesh nor of the will of man, but of God." (Cf. John 8:44, and Romans 8 and 9.)

Involved are the unfathomable issues of election and predestination. For our purpose it can simply be reiterated that God calls his children, and the problem of ultimate identification can then be left in his hands. Perhaps it can be put this way: God calls all human beings (Acts 17:30), but only his children know his voice and respond to his call (John 10:1 – 5). This seems to have been Peter's understanding when he addressed that motley crowd on the Day of Pentecost: "The promise is to you and to your children and to all that are far off, every one whom the Lord our God calls to him" (Acts 2:39).

Some of God's children are indeed far off, and others are near; some are rich, and others are poor; some are well educated, and others are illiterate;

some sweat it out in coal mines, and others analyze charts of production in air-conditioned offices; some tend assembly lines, and others tend babies; some are married, and others are single; some are old, and others are young – yet they are all called with the same call. It is the call to Everyman!

For what purpose does God call? God calls his children to come home (Luke 15:11 – 32), to be faithful members of his household (Eph. 2:19 – 22), to serve him in the orders of his creation (John 17:15 – 19).

In other words, God calls Everyman out of his isolation, alienation, and loneliness into fellowship, into a unique fellowship: "God is faithful, by whom you were called into the fellowship (*koinonia*) of his Son, Jesus Christ our Lord" (1 Cor. 1:9). For this is a fellowship both human and divine: "We have fellowship with one another, and the blood of Jesus his Son cleanses us from all sin" (1 John 1:7). The price of admission into this fellowship is forgiveness, and the price has been paid. Only he who constantly lives in forgiveness is at home in the household of God. And the fellowship of forgiveness is known supremely in the breaking of bread together at the family meal, around the Table of the Lord.

To refer to the fellowship of forgiveness as the household of God is, of course, to use a metaphor to indicate a reality that can never be adequately expressed. Certainly no single metaphor is sufficient in itself to convey the total meaning of the church. Especially illuminating are the metaphors of "the body of Christ" and "the people of God," the former stressing the organic character of the church and the latter the prototype of the church in the people of Israel. Both metaphors emphasize the corporate nature of God's call to Everyman. Christians are "members one of another," be it in a household, a body, or a people.

God calls people, then, to be with him and to be with one another in his household. This is the basic purpose of the divine call, and in a sense it is an "end in itself." But there are errands to be run, functions to be fulfilled, tasks to be done by the various members of the family. To be a member of the household is to have an assignment; both membership and assignment are the gifts of God. Such assignments vary according to (a) the qualifications of the members and (b) their willingness to be of use to the Head of the household.

When God calls Everyman into his family, ipso facto he calls Everyman into the divine service. Everyman's vocation is of one piece, cut from whole cloth. It is a seamless robe, and Everyman will attempt to rend it at his peril. Integral to Everyman's vocation, however, are *two* fields of service—within the household and outside the household—and these fields intersect each other.

This division is made for the purpose of analysis only. In reality we are dealing with the same persons, and with the totality of their lives. The division simply recognizes the fact that these persons, these Christians, are "in the world but not of it," that their "citizenship is in heaven" but presently their lot is cast in "the kingdoms of this world."

Vocation Within the Household

Let it be clear that under this category we shall not be dealing further with the saving action of God by which Everyman is incorporated into his household. We shall be dealing only with the responsibility of Everyman who is already within the community of the called. This responsibility is threefold: to lead a life worthy of the calling, to minister to the saints, and to declare the wonderful deeds of God.

1. *Every Christian is called "to lead a life worthy of the calling to which [he or she] has been called, with all lowliness and meekness, with patience, forbearing one another in love, eager to maintain the unity of the Spirit in the bond of peace"* (Eph. 4:1 – 3).

This familiar passage is illustrative of the extended treatment in the New Testament letters of vocation within the household of faith. It is inconceivable to Paul that members of the body of Christ should lie to one another, steal from one another, slander one another, be covetous of one another, and practice immorality with one another (cf. Colossians 3). On the contrary, within the family all believers should "through love be servants of one another" (Gal. 5:13). Members of a family should be so closely bound together in love that "if one member suffers, all suffer together; if one member is honored, all rejoice together" (1 Cor. 12:26).

The profusion of Pauline teaching on this subject, however, should not make us unmindful of the rich resources in other parts of the New Testament. For example, The First Letter of John could with much justification be given the title of "A Handbook on Vocation Within the Household of Faith." The author does not use the term "vocation" or "calling," but his concern throughout is that the "little children," the members of the family of Christ, should be worthy of the calling to which they have been called. Here is the classic passage:

Beloved, let us love one another; for love is of God, and he who loves is born of God and knows God. He who does not love does not know God; for

God is love. In this the love of God was made manifest among us, that God
sent his only Son into the world, so that we might live through him. In this is
love, not that we loved God but that he loved us and sent his Son to be the
expiation for our sins. Beloved, if God so loved us, we also ought to love one
another. (1 John 4:7 – 11)

The motivation for love within the fellowship of believers has never
been set forth more clearly. That which is at the heart of the biblical
concept of vocation, namely, the divine initiative, is exalted in this passage
as the fountainhead of Christian fellowship.

There have been times and places in the history of the church when
outsiders could point to the family of Christ and say, "How these Christians love one another!" But the record of strife within the visible household of faith is so extensive that it literally fills libraries—both the petty
strife of personal animosities and the bitter theological strife leading to
schism. The disastrous effects of this strife have been as deep as the ocean
and as broad as the sea. Whatever else may be said about these effects, this
can be affirmed: strife within the household of faith is a denial of Christian vocation. For the life we are called to live within the household is one
of lowliness, meekness, patience, forbearing love, eagerness to maintain
the unity of the Spirit in the bond of peace.

2. *Every Christian is called to minister to the saints.* The primary New
Testament word for ministry is *diakonia*, the meaning of which is "service." Translators differ as to how it should be rendered in the many contexts in which it appears. For example, with equal justification Heb. 6:10
can be translated either "to minister to the saints" or "to be of service to
the saints." It is perfectly clear in the New Testament that all members of
the household of God are expected to minister to the saints, i.e., to one
another. This responsibility can be exercised in several ways.

Members of the family are called to minister to the *physical needs* of their
brothers and sisters in Christ. Christians can to some extent carry out a
ministry to physical needs in face-to-face relationships. Within our own
congregations there are always opportunities to minister to those closest
to us. For example, a child who has fallen needs to be picked up; a woman
needs help in the nursing of her aged father; a fellow student needs tutorial
assistance to master a difficult subject; a hospitalized member needs to be
visited. But beyond the immediate reach of their own hands Christians
can greatly extend their ministry by giving financially to the physical relief

and rehabilitation programs of their church. This stewardship of material resources thereby becomes a part of their vocation.

Christians are also called to minister to one another's *spiritual needs*. And so Paul writes to the Colossians (Col. 3:16): "Let the word of Christ dwell in you richly, [as you] teach and admonish one another in all wisdom." Wisdom in spiritual matters is not the exclusive possession of the ordained pastor; neither is the responsibility for teaching and admonishing the members of the household of faith vested only in the clergy. To the Galatians, Paul writes: "Brethren, if a man is overtaken in any trespass, you who are spiritual should restore him in a spirit of gentleness" (Gal. 6:1). Here is a difficult ministry to spiritual needs which, says Paul, can properly be carried out by any member of the household who is sufficiently "spiritual."

All Christians, then, are called to be ministers to one another. This is an integral part of their vocation. Most Christians carry out such a ministry quietly within the limits of their aptitudes, but some Christians receive special gifts which bring their ministry special recognition. And so Paul writes to the Corinthians (1 Corinthians 12) that "there are varieties of gifts, but the same Spirit; and there are varieties of service [ministry], but the same Lord." He proceeds to list eleven specifically identified services rendered in the church. These services should not be performed with a view to honor but rather in such a fashion that all members of the body of Christ "may have the same care for one another." (Special functions and offices in the church will be considered in the next chapter.)

3. *Every Christian is called to declare the wonderful deeds of God.* Addressing the church, the author of 1 Peter asks in effect: Why do you think God has "called you out of darkness into his marvelous light" and has designated you as "a chosen race, a royal priesthood, a holy nation, God's own people" (1 Pet. 2:9)? Answer: "That you may declare the wonderful deeds of him who called you" to those that are still in darkness.

This part of Everyman's vocation in the church merges almost imperceptibly with his vocation in the world. Indeed, it is the point at which the church moves into the world to fulfill its mission there in response to its Lord's command, "You shall be my witnesses in Jerusalem and in all Judea and Samaria and to the end of the earth" (Acts 1:8).

Everyman's vocation within the household of faith is to support the church with prayers and gifts as the church undertakes to carry out its mission of witness in areas where Everyman himself cannot declare the wonderful deeds of God everywhere. Individual Christians can make their witness in their own station in the world, in the place where they are, but Everyman alone cannot directly witness to Christ "to the end of the earth." And so the Christian's vocation, it again appears, includes the stewardship of material resources.

The Spirit of God calls his children by means of the church, to which has been entrusted his Word. On the one hand, there is the *life* of the church, the life within the household nourished by Word and Sacrament; on the other hand, there is the *mission* of the church, which flows from its life into the world. The strength of the church's mission depends upon the vitality of life within the household of faith; and, in turn, the vitality of life within the household depends in no small measure upon the church's acceptance of its mission outside the household.

The mission of the church is a corporate mission. This is said at the risk of redundancy, because the calling of Everyman to declare the wonderful deeds of God must be seen within this corporate mission. As we have noted, this truth becomes obvious when the gifts of one Christian must be joined with the gifts of many other Christians in order to plant the church in some remote corner of the earth. Everyman must also recognize this truth as he or she attempts to declare the deeds of God in the community, in the office, in the factory, in the classroom; for even there Everyman does not make a witness alone or in his or her own strength. In seeking to fulfill this aspect of vocation, Everyman must do so as a member of the body of Christ, within the fellowship of a royal priesthood, undergirded by the prayers of the whole household of God. For Everyman to try to witness to Christ "on his or her own" is to court frustration and defeat, for Everyman's calling to make Christ known is set within the mission of the whole church.

To summarize: Everyman's vocation within the household of faith is to walk worthily of the calling to which he or she has been called, to minister according to his gifts to the physical and spiritual needs of the saints, and to declare either directly or indirectly the wonderful deeds of God.

Vocation Outside the Household

Everyman is called to live both in the church and in the world. A Christian always wrestles with a double temptation: either to identify completely with the world and thereby lose one's soul, or to escape from the world and thereby disclaim human needs and deny the divine command. The call of God does not take Everyman out of the world but places him or her squarely in the world. Christians know, of course, that unless they are constantly being transformed by the renewing of their mind through life in the household of faith, they will inevitably be conformed to the world and fail to fulfill their vocation there.

At the outset let it be bluntly affirmed that according to our Christian understanding *no person has a vocation in the world unless that person has a vocation in the church.* John Smith may have an excellent job, for which he is highly qualified and to which he is completely dedicated, but if God has not called him into the household of faith, John Smith has no vocation. Let it be said with equal bluntness that *vocation cannot be equated with occupation, although vocation may include occupation.* In contrast to any delimitation, let it be affirmed once again that a Christian's vocation includes every facet of life.

Here is Hans Mueller, a mechanic. It so happens that Hans is the son of an immigrant couple, still living; he has recently become a citizen of the United States; he is a member of the local labor union; he is a registered Democrat; he and his wife have been married twelve years, and they have two children; his house is so located that he has three close neighbors; and he is a member of St. Paul's Church on Kensington Avenue. Is Hans's vocation being a mechanic? Not at all! God calls Hans into the household of faith and into his service to be a competent mechanic, a devoted son, a loyal citizen, a responsible member of his labor union and his political party, a faithful husband, a wise father, and a good neighbor. His vocation includes all these established relationships as well as all the casual relationships which vary from day to day.

In all these relationships Everyman is called to glorify God. If "the heavens are telling the glory of God" (Ps. 19:1), certainly Everyman should "ascribe to the Lord the glory due his name" (Ps. 96:8). And this is accomplished not only by bringing an offering and coming into his courts to "worship the Lord in holy array" (Ps. 96:9) but by doing everything to the glory of God (1 Cor. 10:31).

What does the glorification of God mean, then, in terms of Everyman's vocation outside the household of faith?

1. *A Christian's vocation is to glorify God by being of service to all persons regardless of their status.* A Christian is called not only to minister to those of the household of faith but also to serve all people—Jew and Gentile, black

and white, American and non-American. Everyman's vocation in the world is to translate the law of love (Luke 10:27) into "specifics."

In this regard, Everyman's vocation is shaped by the need of one's neighbor. And this includes the total need of the neighbor. An escaped victim of totalitarian terrorism needs to have his wounds cared for, but his need does not end there. Having lost all his material resources, he needs food and shelter, but the matter does not end there. After he has recovered his health, he needs work to do if he is to maintain his self-respect and meet his obligations in society, but the matter does not end there. Even though he is meeting his obligations to society (after a fashion, perhaps!), he still needs to come to terms with his Creator, and to know the peace that passes all understanding. Everyman's vocation is to help one's neighbor meet all these needs, and this involves the whole range of service from social welfare to evangelism. In the words of Paul as addressed to the Corinthians, "Under the test of this service, you will glorify God by your obedience in acknowledging the gospel of Christ, and by the generosity of your contribution for them [the saints] *and for all others*" (2 Cor. 9:13; italics mine).

Everyman is called to serve his or her neighbor not only through monetary contributions and through personal action on behalf of the neighbor's welfare, but also by acting responsibly toward the structures of society. In other words, service to all human beings involves not only social welfare but also *social justice*. Vocation lays upon Everyman, for example, a responsibility both for the victims of totalitarianism and for totalitarianism itself. "This means," in the words of Joseph Sittler,

> that the will to help must devise the means to help in ways determined by the actual collectivities within which men are deepeningly involved, and within which interdependency relates each man to all men by a thousand cords. Needs that are shaped by structures must be met by help that also is structured.[1]

Everyman is called to work for justice, because "justice is a primary instrument of love and a field for its operations."[2]

This implication of Christian vocation, especially for the church, is clearly expressed in the Report of the Fifth Assembly of the World Council of Churches, as follows:

> Whenever a Christian is confronted by the structures of injustice and takes

part in struggles for liberation, he or she is bound to experience the grip of destructive forces which are at work throughout the human family. . . .

The gospel brings us a message of God's total identification with humanity which is suffering under sin and other destructive powers. God's own solidarity with human beings is expressed in the reality of the servant Christ who humbled himself to take up the human form, who was born into poverty, who accepted the path of rejection, and who finally met his death on the cross. . . .

God calls his Church, a community of forgiven sinners, to follow Christ on the same path committed to the cause of the poor, oppressed, and rejected, to declare the love of God by word and by the whole life and to accept the cross.[3]

At this point something must be said about Everyman's responsibility for his or her own physical and mental well-being. Three perversions must be identified and rejected. *First*, there is the view that since we are saved by grace, and only the soul is of importance anyhow, what we do with our bodies is of no great consequence. *Second*, there is the view of the medieval church that bodily discipline is an instrument of salvation: to fast, to scourge oneself, to wear uncomfortable clothes, and to sleep in even more uncomfortable beds accrued to the Christian's celestial credit. *Third*, there is the view of the physical culturists and the intellectual purists that a perfect figure and a razor-sharp mind are their own justification, i.e., figure for figure's sake and mind for mind's sake. Over against these perversions stands the biblical view: in their vocation Christians will care for their body and mind as artisans care for their tools.

2. *A Christian's vocation is to glorify God by making the best possible use of the gifts God has given.* This is applicable, of course, to the use of gifts within as well as outside the household of faith. Everyman should use the special endowments God has given in both realms. In fact, to draw the line between the sacred and the secular is frequently very difficult.

Johann Sebastian Bach wrote all his music *sub specie aeternitatis.* He did not compose to please his benefactors, or to win the plaudits of an audience or of a congregation. At the top of each score he put two sets of initials: S. D. G.—*Soli Deo Gloria*, "to the glory of God alone"; and J. J.— *Jesu juva*, "Help me, Jesus." As Albert Schweitzer points out in his great work on Bach, these initials were to him no mere formulas. "Music is an act of worship with Bach. His artistic activity and his personality are both based on his faith. . . . All great art, even secular, is in itself religious in his eyes; for him the tones do not perish, but ascend to God like praise too deep for utterance." In Bach's own words, music "should have no other end and aim than the glory of God and the re-creation of the soul; where this is not kept in mind there is no true music, but only an infernal clamour and ranting."[4]

Bach is an excellent example of a Christian who in his vocation uses his gifts to the glory of God both in the church and in the world. Whether one is listening to *The Passion According to St. Matthew* or to the *Brandenburg Concertos*, the music seems to "ascend to God like praise too deep for utterance." One senses unmistakably the dimensions of depth and height; one becomes aware of a frame of reference whose parapets are in eternity.

Well, someone may be thinking, that is true enough for Bach, but what about more ordinary mortals? What about Christians whose gifts are in fields such as construction, industry, farming, medicine, government, the fine arts, teaching? How can these persons use their aptitudes, their skills, to the glory of God? This is perhaps the most difficult question in any consideration of vocation in the workaday world. There are no easy answers; in fact, at many points there are no answers—at least not yet. Some things are clear, however, and need to be said.

For one thing, Christians engaged in construction, industry, farming, medicine, government, the fine arts, teaching are *called to glorify God in and through these fields* and not merely in peripheral ways, that is, in ways that have no necessary connection with the fields themselves. Take teaching. Here is a Christian who is a professor of sociology. Note that I did not refer to her as a "Christian teacher." This would have been a misnomer, because she has neatly divided her life into two compartments. As a Christian she feels that she is discharging her responsibilities by ushering once a month at First Church, by serving as adviser to the campus religious council, and by being available to her students for counseling. When she enters the classroom, however, she leaves her Christian faith behind and becomes a naturalist! Christians whose lifework is teaching cannot fulfill their vocation unless they glorify God in and through their teaching. To glorify God their scholarship must, of course, be sound and their pedagogy effective; but beyond that, their teaching must be within a discernible Christian frame of reference.

A second thing that needs to be said about a Christian's making the best possible use of the gifts God has given is this: *piety is no substitute for compe-*

tence. The point has already been implied but it must be made explicit. It is not enough that a Christian engineer be "sincere," a faithful member of St. John's Church by the town hall, and a leader of family worship in his home. A Christian engineer will not glorify God unless he is technically proficient. All the prayers of himself, his family, and St. John's congregation cannot be counted on to save the suspension bridge he designed from collapsing into the river if he has not provided adequately for the stresses and strains of a one-hundred-mile-an-hour wind! Not to be competent is both an affront to the Creator who endowed him with gifts and a callous betrayal of his neighbors whom he is called to serve in love.

Closely related to the question of competence is the matter of *integrity*, especially in the arts and crafts. God's creative gifts can be used to his glory only if the work of artists and artisans reveals an essential honesty, an inner truthfulness. God desires "truth in the inward being," as the psalmist says (Ps. 51:6), and without this truth in the arts and crafts God is not being glorified. The creative gifts bestowed by God are so easily and so frequently prostituted to ignoble ends. When artists and artisans create what the public wants rather than what they know is sound; when they use their gifts to produce what will sell rather than what is honest; when they yield to pressures for that which is cheap, artificial, and hollow—then is integrity forfeited, and Christians who yield to such temptations have to that extent failed in their vocation.

3. *A Christian's vocation to glorify God must be grounded in God's command and renewed by his grace.* To put it another way, only by divine command and by divine grace can a Christian have a vocation in the world. Here we are deeply indebted to Luther for establishing the only basis upon which Everyman can be in the world and not of it. Let us recall his concept of the two realms (see pp. 46 – 47).

A Christian lives in two realms, in two dimensions—the dimension of grace and the dimension of law. In the *realm of grace*, Everyman is given the pure righteousness of Christ and the unqualified freedom of the sons of God. This is the realm of absolutes, the dimension of perfection. Here the only compulsion is the constraint of the love of Christ. In the *realm of law*, only "civil" righteousness can be realized, and Everyman's freedoms are severely limited. This is the realm of relativities, of compromise, of rough justice. Without external compulsion, anarchy would prevail. Both realms belong to God, and to both the forgiven sinner belongs.

As Christians seek to fulfill their vocation outside the household of faith, they must remember that they really are in the world. They must accept their place in the orders of creation and be subject to the compulsions of these orders. What is more, as Christians seek to serve others in the structures of these orders, they will be required to effect compromises (viewed in the light of absolutes) that greater evil may not prevail.

Therefore it is affirmed that Everyman can play his or her role in society, and especially in the political and economic orders, only because of the command of God and the grace of God. On the one hand, it is God's will that the orders of creation be maintained, and that Everyman accept a proper share of responsibility to uphold these orders. On the other hand, when Everyman in government or in industry commits evil that greater evil may not prevail, the evil done is still evil, and must be forgiven if Everyman is to live also in the realm of grace. The forgiveness of God not only cleanses the hands of his servants doing his work in the world; it also "lets loose" in the world through these servants fresh streams of renewal and creativity.

One of the great contributions that Gustaf Wingren has made to our understanding of Christian vocation is at this point. Although he demonstrates in a masterful way the necessity of distinguishing between the two realms, he writes as follows:

> Love born of faith and the Spirit effects a complete breakthrough of the boundary between the two kingdoms, the wall of partition between heaven and earth, as did God's incarnation in Christ. . . . Faith transfers to love the freedom from law it had in heaven, so that love on earth carries with it faith's own freedom from law. . . . God descends from heaven and transforms the earth, now here, now there, as faith and love appear through the church's preaching of the gospel, through the spiritual realm. The task of the church includes a continuing renewal of the worldly orders, a never-ending alertness in all vocations, from the princely to the meanest labor.[5]

Everyman's exercise of vocation is pedestrian so much of the time, motivated by obligation and mellowed by the divine consolation; but when the flame of faith burns brightly and the spirit breaks through the crust of routine experience, then Everyman's vocation takes wings and each moment is transfigured with joy.

To summarize: Everyman's vocation outside the household of faith involves the perennial task of glorifying God in every facet of life. Vocation summons Everyman to glorify God through loving service to all persons; it challenges Everyman to make the most fruitful use of the gifts God has given; and it equips Everyman by divine command and grace to be effectively instrumental to God in the realization of his purposes for the whole creation.

Living in Vocation

We come finally to the questions: How can Everyman live in his or her vocation? How can vocation come alive for Everyman? How can the call from God lay hold upon Everyman in such a compelling way that one's entire existence is transformed? Here are five simple but basic suggestions addressed not to the unbeliever but to *Everyman who is already a member of the household of faith and yet for whom vocation is unreal.* They are addressed to the person who can honestly confess: "The Holy Spirit has called me by the Gospel . . . even as He calls, gathers, enlightens, and sanctifies the whole Church." And they are addressed to Everyman personally.

1. *Be a faithful member of the household of God*

Here your vocation began, and this is where it must take roots and grow. The sense of vocation is strong in proportion to the strength of faith, and faith is fed by Word and Sacrament. Without the Word of forgiveness and the sacramental fellowship in the family of Christ faith will wither like a plant deprived of water, and the sense of vocation will grow dim. Living vocation means constancy in the hearing of the Word and in the reception of the Sacrament of the Lord's Supper.

It also means accepting your responsibilities within the household of God—to love and honor members of the family of Christ, to minister as you can to their several needs, and to share with them the mission of the church to make Christ known to the end of the earth. As you fulfill this part of your vocation within the household of faith, you may expect to see your vocation outside the household of faith take on meaning and power.

2. *Respond in obedience to the claims God makes upon your life.*

You know very well some of the claims God is making upon your life at this moment. Respond in obedience. God's call will be heard in more and more of your activities and relationships as you respond in obedience to those claims which are now unmistakably clear. If you are obedient in one task, God will call you to another task, and as you are obedient in many tasks assurance of vocation will grow. But how does God reveal his will for each member of his household? How does he make his claims known?

Einar Billing would reply that God reveals his will in the forgiveness of sins. "It is worthy of note," he says, "that the forgiveness of sins gives not only the motive and power to accomplish a deed already planned, but it gives first of all the deed itself, that is, clarity as to what deed God desires of me."[6] Gustaf Wingren would reply that God makes his claims known in the context of persons and events in which we live. This is the way he puts it: "God does not come to man in thoughts and feelings which well up in him when he isolates himself from the world, but rather in what happens to man in the external and tangible events which take place about him."[7] Whether God lays his claims upon you through the forgiveness of sin or through people and events (and he does both), obedience is a condition of your continuing to hear his voice.

3. *Rejoice in your present station in life but do not accept it as final.*

Although your station in life may be far from ideal, be grateful that you do have a place in God's world and that he has given you neighbors to serve. On the other hand, never regard your station in life as final. Christians live in a dynamic world and serve a creative God. Just as we are pilgrims on earth, so we are pilgrims in our stations in life. Some stations are more stable than others, but the stability of no station is absolutely assured. The phenomenon of physical mobility in America gives new meaning to the ancient word, "Here we have no lasting city" (Heb. 13:14)! As the world's needs change, and as your qualifications change (for better or for worse), the shape of your vocation in the world is subject to change. What God wills for you today may not be what he wills for you tomorrow.

Therefore, both acceptance and openness are necessary if your vocation is to remain alive. You must accept your present station and, so far as possible, live in it to the glory of God; at the same time, you must be open to the call of God to serve him in new ways or in different circumstances. Part of this openness is constant willingness to prepare yourself for service more fully commensurate with your God-given talents. If you are now a student, remember that preparation in itself is just as much vocation under God as being the physician you hope someday to be. Stations may change, but vocation is continuous. Christians may leave their station in life, but they cannot leave their vocation—and still be Christian.

4. *Grow in your knowledge of yourself and of the various fields of your vocation.*

God gave you your vocation, but he did not give you (by revelation!) the factual knowledge necessary to translate your calling into effective action both within the household of faith and outside the household. In all the roles you are called upon to play—whether of engineer or of sister or of spouse or of citizen—you are under obligation to equip yourself to play the roles well. Failure to do so may very well result in a state of confusion and uncertainty regarding your calling. Growth in knowledge about the various fields of your vocation should always be accompanied by a comparable growth in knowledge about yourself. If your understanding of yourself is superficial or inaccurate, your whole vocation can take on a semblance of unreality.

This mandate applies also to the young man or woman wrestling with the problem of what his or her lifework ought to be. To participation in the community of believers, obedience to the divine commands, and gratitude for opportunities of immediate service should be added careful evaluation of personal aptitudes and of human needs. Testing, consultation with experts, and study of possible fields of labor all have their proper places in the unfolding of divine will for a person standing on the threshold of life. No Christian will ever regard these techniques as being autonomous, as alone constituting sufficient guidance, but they can be used by God to help reveal his purposes. To neglect them would be as irresponsible as the attempt of a surgeon to perform a difficult operation without making use of the best available instruments.

5. *Pray for God's guidance and help in every aspect of your vocation.*

Prayer is, of course, no substitute for obedience to divine commands. If you are not responding daily to the unmistakable claims that God is making upon your life, the feeling of unreality about your vocation will not be remedied simply by praying. On the other hand, obedience divorced from prayer degenerates into mere legalism, and legalism is just about as deadly as disobedience. The common temptation of Christians is to make their decisions and to attempt to carry out their plans without bothering to consult the King of creation either because of sheer indifference and lack of faith or because they are consciously or unconsciously evading God, whose commands they would rather not hear.

If you believe that God is, that he cares, that you are a member of his own household by virtue of his personal call, then how ridiculous it is that you should hesitate to speak with him frankly about your vocation. "Ask, and it will be given you; seek, and you will find; knock, and it will be opened to you. For every one who asks receives, and he who seeks finds, and to him who knocks it will be opened" (Luke 11:9 – 10). This is the promise of your Lord.

Living in vocation, then, is living in the household of God, the family of Christ, the holy catholic church; it is living in obedience to God in all things, both great and small; it is living in gratitude for what God has given and in openness for whatever he has in store; it is living in commitment to grow in understanding of self and of one's fields of service; it is living in the posture of prayer so that God may always have free access to the innermost soul. So to live is to know with exceeding great joy the vocation God has in store for Everyman.

5

VOCATION AS MINISTRY

God calls his children into the household of faith and to loving service both in the church and in the world. This is the vocation of Everyman. It involves both *being* and *doing*. The vocation of Everyman begins by being called into and by being nurtured in the household of faith, and that vocation continues in Everyman's service or ministry to members of the household and indeed to all human beings in need. Every Christian is a minister!

As the twentieth century comes to a close this truth of the Christian faith is affirmed almost everywhere in the churches. This was not the case a quarter of a century ago when "minister" was a term used to designate a member of the clergy. Although this way of thinking had been emerging for some time, the Second Vatican Council marked a highly significant watershed between two eras of theological reflection. By 1982 the World Council of Churches' Faith and Order Commission statement, *Baptism, Eucharist, and Ministry,* could declare with almost no challenge that "the word *ministry* in its broadest sense denotes the service to which the whole people of God is called, whether as individuals, as a local community, or as the universal Church."[1] Baptism is every Christian's call to ministry under the Lordship of Christ.

Because of the shift in theological thinking about the general ministry of the church there has been a universal recognition of the crucial role of the laity in the life of the people of God. The growth of lay participation in the worship of the church has been phenomenal. Laymen and laywomen have had an increasing share in decision-making on all levels of church life. In 1958, Hendrik Kraemer pioneered in producing *A Theology of the Laity*[2] which spawned a succession of articles and volumes on the same theme. The laity had finally come into its own.

Unfortunately, this emergence of the laity in the ministry of the church has had two unfortunate consequences. In the first place, the root meaning of the word *laos*, referring to the *whole* people of God, tended to be supplanted by a restrictive usage carrying the implication of "nonclergy." Lay participation in the worship, the decision-making, and the witness of the church has frequently come to mean nonclerical participation. Second, because of the growing emphasis upon the call of every member of the household of God to minister, the distinctive role of the *ordained* minister has become increasingly confused. Is there *any* function in the ministry of the church that *only* the *ordained* minister is authorized to perform? Even baptism, usually in an emergency situation, can be performed by any Christian and so programmed is almost universally accepted as valid. Likewise, many church bodies will authorize a nonordained person, under certain circumstances, to celebrate the Eucharist. No wonder the called clergy has a problem of identification.

In our search for the meaning of the Christian's calling we began with the Scriptures, because for the Christian there is no other place to begin. So, in our consideration of vocation as service, as ministry, let us begin with the New Testament. That the Christian's calling eventuates in ministry is abundantly clear. But how is this ministry to be understood in the ordering of the life and mission of the church?

Ministry in the New Testament

Ministry in the New Testament is, of course, a very extensive and generally obscure subject. Over the centuries the most brilliant scholars have been unable to settle the issues, and the most illustrious church councils have been unable to resolve the differences of interpretation. My aim here is to state a point of view.

As already noted in chapter 4, the primary New Testament word for ministry is *diakonia*, the literal meaning of which is "service" (in classical Greek the serving of food or drink). Translators differ as to how it should be rendered in the various contexts. For example, the King James Version translates Matt. 20:28 as follows: "The Son of man came not to be ministered unto but to minister." The Revised Standard Version, however, reads as follows: "The Son of man came not to be served but to serve." The Greek words in question are passive and active forms, respectively, of the verb *diakonein*, "to serve." It is both a technical and a subjective matter to decide when *diakonia* should be translated "ministry" and when "service."

Another New Testament word for ministry is *leitourgia*, which in classical Greek means a service rendered to the state, usually at a person's own expense. In the Revised Standard Version, *leitourgia* (and its related forms) is variously translated as "ministry," "service," "worship," "sacrifice," and the like. For example, Heb. 8:6 is rendered, "Christ has obtained a ministry (*leitourgias*) which is as much more excellent than the old as the covenant he mediates is better, since it is enacted on better promises" (cf. Rom. 15:16 or Phil. 2:25). On the other hand, 2 Cor. 9:12 is translated, "For the rendering of this service (*leitourgias*) not only supplies the wants of the saints but also overflows in many thanksgivings to God" (cf. Luke 1:23 or Phil. 2:30). Again, determination of meaning in each instance is both a technical and a subjective matter.

An examination of the uses of *diakonia* and *leitourgia* must be supplemented, of course, by a comprehensive study of the church in the New Testament before an understanding can be reached as to the nature of the ministry in the New Testament. Such an approach, I believe, leads to the following conclusions:

1. *Ministry is a general, rather than a restrictive, concept and includes a variety of services.*

In the fourth chapter of the letter to the Ephesians the unity of the church is stressed in terms of its being "one body and one Spirit" and having "one Lord, one faith, one baptism," and then the letter goes on to say that "grace was given to each of us according to the measure of Christ's gifts. . . . And his gifts were that some should be apostles, some prophets, some evangelists, some pastors and teachers, *to equip the saints for the work of ministry, for building up the body of Christ,* until we all attain to the unity of the faith and of the knowledge of the Son of God, to mature manhood, to the measure of the stature of the fulness of Christ" (Eph. 4:7, 11 – 13; italics mine). It is important to note that in this passage "the work of ministry" appears to be synonymous with "to equip the saints" and "for building up the body of Christ"—also descriptive phrases of a general nature. Apostles, prophets, evangelists, pastors, and teachers all share in this ministry; no one category of service can claim the ministry for its own.

This understanding receives extended support in the well-known twelfth chapter of 1 Corinthians where Paul affirms that "there are varieties of service" (*diakonion*), which can be just as well translated "there are varieties of ministry" (1 Cor. 12:5). He then proceeds to list eleven different "workings" in the body of Christ, including not only prophecy and teaching but also performing miracles, healing, speaking in tongues, and simply helping.

These passages in Ephesians and 1 Corinthians are further corroborated in the twelfth chapter of Romans (especially vv. 4 – 8). Paul describes Christians as members of the body of Christ, each member having a different function according to the gifts of the Spirit. It is significant that his illustrative list of functions includes not only prophecy, teaching, and exhortation but also contributing funds, giving aid, and doing acts of mercy.

2. *Ministry, being of a general and inclusive nature, belongs to the body of Christ as a whole.*

Ministry is not the exclusive prerogative of the apostles, even though the apostles are the members of the household of faith who are held in the highest regard. Jesus himself chose the Twelve, but the Twelve do not lay exclusive claim to ministry. Neither is it affirmed in the later New Testament writings that ministry is entirely in the hands of elders or of bishops.

This is true because no one member of the household of faith, and no small coterie of members, possesses all the gifts of the Spirit. These gifts are distributed among many different members, from the lowliest to the highest, each member performing a function for which he is peculiarly qualified. This is not to say that several functions cannot occasionally be performed by one person, as was certainly the case in the primitive church and has been the case in succeeding centuries.

Not only does ministry belong to the whole body of Christ; the whole body of Christ bears responsibility for ministry, so that "all things should be done decently and in order" (1 Cor. 14:40). Without order the rich and diverse manifestations of the Spirit result in chaos in the household of God.

3. *Through the church God calls all members of the body of Christ to minister to one another.*

Within the household of faith there is a mutual ministry, as already noted in chapter 4. This ministry can take place in the public assemblies of the believers, where different members make contributions according to their gifts. This ministry can also be exercised outside the assemblies in personal relationships between believers.

This mutual ministry is directed to both physical and spiritual needs, as we have seen. Gifts are sent not only to congregations in need but also to individuals, such as Paul in prison. And within each congregation members certainly ministered to one another's physical needs. A mutual ministry was also carried on in terms of spiritual needs, and this involved teaching, admonishing, and restoration to the fellowship of the household.

As Christians minister to one another, especially in the spiritual realm, they are manifesting in one way the priesthood of all believers, a much misunderstood concept. No believer is a priest in isolation from other believers. This teaching of the New Testament cannot be viewed simply as "the right of the individual to approach God directly." The doctrine of the priesthood of all believers is based on five passages (1 Pet. 2:4 – 5; 2:9 – 10; Rev. 1:5 – 6; 5:9 – 10; 20:6), and all five passages refer to the priesthood in a corporate rather than in an individual sense. All members of the household of God together constitute "a holy priesthood," or "a royal priesthood," which they exercise on behalf of Christ, the great and final High Priest. Each believer can exercise a priestly function in relation to his or her fellow believers, and believers together as the body of Christ can exercise a priestly function in relation to the world.

4. *Through the church God calls certain members to perform special offices or assignments on behalf of the whole body of Christ.*

Accordingly, the church at a very early stage in its history designated seven members to assume special responsibility for the distribution of food to the believers. Said the Twelve: "Pick out from among you seven men of good repute, full of the Spirit and of wisdom, whom we may appoint to this duty." After the whole body of the disciples had made the selection, we read that "these they set before the apostles, and they prayed and laid their hands upon them" (Acts 6:1 – 6). Likewise, the Book of Acts relates that "while [the believers] were worshiping the Lord and fasting, the Holy Spirit said, 'Set apart for me Barnabas and Saul for the work to which I have called them.' Then after fasting and praying they laid their hands on them and sent them off" (Acts 13:2 – 3). It is important to note that the church's responsibility to designate persons for special assignments or offices can be exercised through persons who had already received the church's approbation (cf. Titus 1:5).

Those designated for special offices or assignments were sometimes formally commissioned or ordained with prayer and the laying on of hands and sometimes they apparently were not so authorized. This formal action does not seem to be restricted to those occupying what might be called "major offices." For example, no member of the church seems to have been formally authorized to govern. John McKenzie, in his very clear and forthright discussion of "Ministerial Structures in the New Testament," also points out that "there is no one . . . to whom the cultic ministry is officially and exclusively committed." Such cultic rites certainly included Baptism, Eucharist, and public common prayer.[3] Indeed, information in the New Testament about special offices and assignments is remarkably ambiguous and sketchy. By the beginning of the second century the titles of deacon, presbyter, and bishop had gained rather wide usage, but the titles of priest and pope do not appear in the New Testament. John McKenzie well summarizes the whole matter in these words:

> It is obvious that pluriform structure is general in the New Testament. Nothing suggests a uniform structure imposed from above. This does not imply that development beyond the New Testament is impossible or undesirable; it does imply that such a development, when it occurred, was based on other than biblical reasons. To the degree to which these reasons were historical other structures can be suggested by other historical reasons.[4]

Ministry in the Church Today

Of basic importance in any consideration of ministry in the church today is the 1982 Lima text of the *Baptism, Eucharist, and Ministry* report of the Faith and Order Commission of the World Council of Churches. This text is the end product of more than fifty years of work by the Commission and "represents the significant theological convergence which Faith and Order has discerned and formulated."[5] The text, of course, does not yet represent a consensus, "understood as that experience of life and articulation of faith necessary to realize and maintain the Church's visible unity."[6] It is significant that "the Commission also includes among its full members theologians of the Roman Catholic and other churches which do not belong to the World Council of Churches itself."[7] In other words, *Baptism, Eucharist, and Ministry* is the most recent and most widely based ecumenical pronouncement on the subject of ministry in the church today. What does the Lima text say?

1. *God calls the whole people of God into his ministry "to proclaim and prefigure the Kingdom of God."* The church "accomplishes this by announcing the Gospel to the world and by its very existence as the body of Christ."[8] This ministry includes spiritual and physical service to all God's creatures in need, but especially the sinners, the poor, the captives, the disabled, and the oppressed.[9] Christ himself provides the model for such a ministry—the

sacrificial servant (Mark 10:45; Luke 22:27). "This mission needs to be carried out in varying political, social, and cultural contexts. In order to fulfill this mission faithfully, [the members of Christ's body] will seek relevant forms of witness and service in each situation."[10]

2. *Simultaneously with his call to all members of the body of Christ, God calls specific members to special roles and offices, and bestows upon these members gifts (charisma) appropriate to their responsibilities, including the preaching of the Word and the celebrating of the Sacraments as the church's guardians of the faith.* "The Spirit is the giver of diverse gifts which enrich the life of the community. In order to enhance their effectiveness, the community will recognize publicly certain of these charisms. . . . The ordained ministry, which is itself a charism, must not become a hindrance for the variety of these charisms."[11] The call to these distinctive responsibilities is not derived from God's call to the whole people of God, and neither does this call to distinctive responsibilities have precedence over the general call to all members of the body of Christ. The general call and the specific call to ministry come from God himself. "Since the ordained ministry and the community are inextricably related, all members participate in fulfilling these functions. . . . The ordained ministry fulfills these functions in a representative way."[12]

3. *Persons called by God through the church to preach the gospel, celebrate the Sacraments, and guard the historic faith are ordained by "the invocation of the Spirit and the laying on of hands.*[13] In this rite the ordained minister receives the charism (1 Tim. 4:14) which sets him apart and which abides with him forever. Ordination, like baptism, is not repeated. Ordained ministry "is constitutive for the life and witness of the Church."[14]

> As Christ chose and sent the apostles, Christ continues through the Holy Spirit to choose and call persons into the ordained ministry. As heralds and ambassadors, ordained ministers are representatives of Jesus Christ to the community, and proclaim his message of reconciliation. As leaders and teachers they call the community to submit to the authority of Jesus Christ, the teacher and prophet, in whom law and prophets were fulfilled. As pastors, under Jesus Christ the chief shepherd, they assemble and guide the dispersed people of God, in anticipation of the coming Kingdom.[15]

4. *Lay members and ordained members of the believing community are mutually dependent upon one another.* Lay ministers cannot serve Christ without the ministry of Word and Sacrament. Ordained ministers need

"the recognition, the support, and the encouragement of the community."[16] The chief task of the laity is to make an effective witness in the world. "The chief responsibility of the ordained ministry is to assemble and build up the body of Christ by proclaiming and teaching the Word of God, by celebrating the Sacraments, and by guiding the life of the community in its worship, its mission, and its caring ministry."[17]

5. *Since there is not a single pattern of the ordained ministry in the New Testament, a variety of forms and titles has appeared over the centuries.* Nevertheless, the threefold pattern of bishop, presbyter, and deacon seems to have received the most general and widespread usage. Even within this threefold pattern there have been changes in the meaning of the offices and their relationships. It is conceivable that a universal return to the threefold pattern of ministry may be not only possible but also beneficial in terms of the impetus it would give to the movement toward unity. It is suggested that, with the return to the threefold pattern, the titles could very well carry the following meanings and functions:

a. "*Bishops* preach the Word, preside at the sacraments, and administer discipline in such a way as to be representative pastoral ministers of oversight, continuity, and unity in the Church."[18]

b. "*Presbyters* serve as pastoral ministers of Word and Sacraments in a local eucharistic community."[19]

c. "*Deacons* represent to the Church its calling as servant in the world."[20]

These points of convergence in the churches' understanding of ministry are impressive reasons for thanksgiving throughout Christendom. The progress made over the past fifty or more years in ecumenical dialogue and collaboration, especially in the area of ministry, deserves hearty commendation. Nevertheless, there remain subjects about which there are wide divergences of judgment. One of these is the whole matter of apostolic succession. On the one hand, there are churches that regard apostolic succession in the traditional sense as being nonnegotiable. On the other hand, there are churches that argue that the treasures of the apostolic faith can be sufficiently guaranteed without insisting on the traditional succession. Another still bitterly debated matter is the ordination of women, the positions ranging all the way from absolute disapproval through impatient indifference to already existing approval. Still another area of differences in understanding and judgment is the matter of ordination itself. Here the spectrum of differences, both within and between the churches, stretches from a purely functional view to a strictly ontological view, with various mediating proposals being offered in the hope that somehow the existing confusion vis-à-vis ordination can be transcended. And there are still other divergences most of which are susceptible of resolution given sufficient time, patience, theological ingenuity, and forgiving love.

In addition to the staggering achievement of the Faith and Order Commission in its report on *Baptism, Eucharist, and Ministry*, there have been impressive contributions to theological understanding in these and other critical areas from the major traditions through semiofficial bilateral dialogues, official actions of the churches, and the publication of monographs, jointly edited or authored books, and scores of articles in scholarly and ecclesiastical journals. A few of the outstanding thematic editions of such journals dealing with the ministry of the church are listed in the Selected Bibliography at the end of this book.

This is a brief sketch of the ecumenical picture of ministry in the church today. Let us focus now on two of the most pressing issues seen from the perspective of the Christian's calling.

Distinguishing the Roles of Clergy and Laity

It has already been indicated in this chapter that ministry in the New Testament is a general rather than a restrictive concept and includes a great variety of services, not only preaching and teaching but also administering, healing, doing welfare work, speaking in tongues, making financial contributions, and simply helping. The Holy Spirit pours out gifts to members of the household of faith so that these services can be provided. Very early in the history of the Christian community it became necessary for the Twelve to appoint, with the help of the community, the Seven to take over the specific responsibility for the distribution of food. This differentiation of function meant that there were two recognized roles in the primitive church, the Twelve (apostles) and the Seven (deacons). Further differentiation eventually recognized elders, presbyters, bishops, and the like. And the question must have arisen sooner or later, What is the distinctive responsibility of each office? The question is still with us today, especially with reference to the distinctive roles of laity and clergy.

In raising this question, we are not using *laos* as the whole people of God but rather in the popular sense of the nonclergy. God calls the whole people of God into his service, and so every Christian is a minister. Nothing is so widely accepted as this recognition by the churches. All Christians have a ministry to one another in the church, and this includes clerical as well as nonclerical members. It is also widely accepted that clerical members, as guardians of the faith, carry special responsibility for the ministry of Word and Sacrament, i.e., for preaching the Word and celebrating Baptism and Eucharist regardless of the title the office bears in a particular tradition. Despite these acceptances, confusion has been growing in the church over the issue of proper roles. This confusion has been due partly to the increasing emphasis upon the crucial role of the laity in the church and partly to the widespread practice of appointing clergy to positions in the church and outside the church that have very little or nothing to do with the ministry of Word and Sacrament.

Of course, it is well known that contemporary clergy in their parishes are engaged in far more functions than preaching the Word and celebrating the Sacraments. The ordained minister is expected to be something of an expert in public relations, fund-raising, counseling, group therapy, conflict resolution, office management, and general administration, so that H. Richard Niebuhr seriously proposed that the most appropriate title for the contemporary man (or woman) of the cloth ought to be "pastoral director." Nevertheless, we must also take seriously the judgment of the Faith and Order Commission that "the chief responsibility of the ordained ministry is to assemble and build up the body of Christ by proclaiming and teaching the Word of God, by celebrating the sacraments, and by guiding the life of the community in its worship, its mission, and its caring ministry."[21]

The reverse is true with regard to the church's task of evangelism and service in the world. Here the major responsibility must be borne directly by the laity of the church. Witness must be indigenous if it is to be of maximum effectiveness. *Christ can best be made known in all walks of life by those who are identified with these walks of life.* If the gospel is to penetrate the labor unions, it must be carried there by Christians who are bona fide and active members of the union. If the gospel is to penetrate the managerial level of industry, it must be carried there by Christians who have status on that level. If the gospel is to penetrate the university, it must be carried there by Christians who as students, teachers, administrators are natives of the academic community. If the gospel is to penetrate the inner chambers of government, it must be carried there by Christians who command respect as members of the Senate, the State Department, or the White House staff. In relation to these highly important segments of contemporary life ordained ministers are outsiders; they don't belong. The only way that the church can fulfill its mission in relation to labor, to industrial management, to higher education, to government, and to other aspects of culture is through laymen and laywomen who are insiders, who do belong.

What, then, is the role of the clergy with regard to the church's task of evangelism and service in the world? *The role of the clergy is to prepare and support the laity as they discharge their direct responsibility to witness in the secular world.* The effectiveness of lay witness and service depends to a very great degree upon how well this role is played. When it comes to evangelism the clergy are not on the front lines; they are behind the lines giving themselves to "the equipment of the saints" before they go into battle and to "the refreshment of the saints" as they return from the fray confused and exhausted.

And how do the clergy carry out their role of equipping and refreshing the saints? They do so by providing a ministry of Word and Sacrament, a ministry of pastoral care, a ministry of teaching, a ministry of training in "strategy and tactics."

With reference to the mission of the church in the world, ordained clergy have usually conceived their role to be that of exhortation and direct action. On the one hand, they have exhorted laity from the pulpit to be Christian in their daily life and work, and they have frequently done this in ways that do not get at the basic issues which confront laypersons in the secular world. And when occasionally the basic issues are identified, little or no guidance is offered as to how the laity can come to grips with the issues in relation to the Christian faith. So often the consciences of the laity have been disturbed without any constructive action taking place on the front lines. On the other hand, so often the clergy, noting the weakness of lay witness in the world and having a high regard for their own competence, have themselves attempted to penetrate the secular orders. Neither pulpit exhortation alone nor direct clerical action will yield significant gains in the workaday world for the gospel of Christ.

What is needed is a new understanding of the roles of the laity and of the clergy in the mission of the church. The laity have frequently been "inspired" but not equipped for battle; and the clergy have frequently dissipated their energies in frustrating forays into the secular world when they should have been preparing the laity for conquests on terrain the laity already know well. The proper role of the laity in a congregation is not to assist the pastor; the proper role of the pastor is to assist the laity to be the church militant. When laymen and laywomen assemble at the church facilities during the week, it should not be for the purpose of being preached at yet again or of being entertained, but for the purpose of undergoing serious training as witnesses of Christ and of realistically devising strategies for consolidating victories won or for establishing new beachheads on behalf of the church in our communities and in our culture.

Extending Ordination for Additional Functions

As noted above, *Baptism, Eucharist, and Ministry* strongly urges the churches to affirm the threefold pattern of the ordained ministry—bishop, presbyter, and deacon—because of its already wide usage in Christendom, its appearance in the New Testament, and its usefulness in the search for unity in the churches today. This could well be another major convergence in the realm of ecumenical theology. For many churches this step would require approval of the ordination, in some form, of deacons.

The document suggests that the threefold pattern of the ordained ministry be further delineated as follows:

> *Bishops* preach the Word, preside at the sacraments, and administer discipline in such a way as to be representative pastoral ministers of oversight, continuity, and unity in the Church. They have pastoral oversight of the area to which they are called. They serve the apostolicity and unity of the Church's teaching, worship, and sacramental life. They have responsibility for leadership in the Church's mission. They relate the Christian community in their area to the wider church, and the universal Church to their community. They, in communion with the presbyters and deacons and the whole community, are responsible for the orderly transfer of ministerial authority in the Church.
>
> *Presbyters* serve as pastoral ministers of Word and Sacraments in a local eucharistic community. They are preachers and teachers of the faith, exercise

pastoral care, and bear responsibility for the discipline of the congregation to the end that the world may believe and that the entire membership of the Church may be renewed, strengthened, and equipped in ministry. Presbyters have particular responsibility for the preparation of members for Christian life and ministry.

Deacons represent to the Church its calling as servant in the world. By struggling in Christ's name with the myriad needs of societies and persons, deacons exemplify the interdependence of worship and service in the Church's life. They exercise responsibility in the worship of the congregation: for example, by reading the Scriptures, preaching, and leading people in prayer. They help in the teaching of the congregation. They exercise a ministry of love within the community. They fulfill certain administrative tasks and may be elected to responsibilities for governance.[22]

The descriptions of all three offices are given so that the delineation of the office of deacon may be seen in perspective along with the other two offices. Our concern at this point, however, is not with building a case either for or against the office of deacon. Certainly the proposal of a three-fold pattern for the ordained ministry deserves careful study by the churches as well as by the Faith and Order Commission. It is highly significant that the Roman Catholic Church is in the process of reactivating the permanent diaconate and that other communions (e.g., Episcopalians and Methodists) which include the office of deacon in their orders have been reexamining their understanding of the diaconate.

Since it is proposed that deacons be ordained along with presbyters and bishops, the wording of paragraph 46 *of Baptism, Eucharist, and Ministry* should be noted: "Ordained persons may be professional ministers in the sense that they receive their salaries from the church. The church may also ordain people who remain in other occupations or employment."[23] This suggestion poses questions especially as applied to the office of deacon but also as applied to parish pastors. But such questions will receive no consideration here.

The issue raised in this section has to do with the "job description" of the office of deacon. Should the office of deacon be limited to the functions described in the document? Or should the office of deacon be conceived broadly enough so as to include a wide variety of services as indicated in the New Testament or as reflected in existing "church occupations" today?

As noted several times in this book, ministry in the New Testament includes a variety of services. "Grace was given to each of us according to the measure of Christ's gift. . . . And his gifts were that some should be apostles, some prophets, some evangelists, some pastors and teachers" (Ephesians 4). Paul in 1 Corinthians 12 lists eleven gifts of the Spirit, including the roles of apostles, prophets, teachers, miracle workers, healers, helpers, administrators, and speakers in various kinds of tongues. In his letter to the Romans he adds to the list those who contribute funds and those who perform acts of mercy. How many of these persons, if any, received public recognition as deacons?

Or consider the astonishing variety of so-called church occupations today: organist, choir director, director of Christian education, director of youth work, parish worker, parochial school teacher, college or seminary faculty member, writer, editor, group work expert, secretary, receptionist, nurse, social worker, business manager, administrator, and the like. Assuming that all these employed persons are members of the household of faith, and, further, that they regard what they do in their jobs as part and parcel of their Christian vocation, what claim, if any, do they have to be considered for ordination to the office of deacon?

In a word, should ordination be extended to include functions other than those primarily identified with the offices of bishop and presbyter? It has been suggested that the diaconate include not only those responsibilities traditionally assigned to the office but also those of teaching in the church school, in the parochial school, and even in the church college and seminary. It has also been suggested that the diaconate be extended to cover certain special ministries outside the parish, such as to the Armed Forces, hospitals and rehabilitation centers, and secular college and university campuses.

Looked at from the historical perspective, it would appear that (in the language of *Baptism, Eucharist, and Ministry*) just as bishops have been regarded as "representative pastoral ministers of oversight, continuity, and unity in the Church" and presbyters as "pastoral ministers of Word and Sacraments in a local eucharistic community," so have deacons been expected to "represent to the Church its calling as servant in the world." This emphasis upon *the deacon's servanthood in the world* appears not only in the language of the document but also in the language of the diaconal ordination rites of particular church bodies.

In the Episcopal rite, for example, the bishop addresses the ordinand as follows: "God now calls you to a special ministry of servanthood directly under your bishop. In the name of Jesus Christ, you are to serve all people, particularly the poor, the weak, the sick, and the lonely. . . . You are to assist the bishop and priests in public worship and in the ministration of God's Word and Sacraments. . . . At all times, your life and teaching are to show Christ's people that in serving the helpless they are serving Christ himself."[24]

In the proposed United Methodist rite the bishop addresses the ordinand as follows: "God has called you to a special ministry that will exemplify this servanthood in the Church and in the world. In the name of Jesus Christ, you are to serve all people, particularly the poor, the weak, the sick, and the lonely. You are to represent to the Church the ministry of servanthood in the world to which all Christians are called in baptism. . . . At all times, by your life and teaching you are to show Christ's people that in serving the helpless they are serving Christ."[25]

It is important to note the similarity of the *Baptism, Eucharist, and Ministry* wording, the Episcopal rite, the proposed United Methodist rite, and the 1980 edition of the statement on "Ministry" of the Consultation on Church Union. Here is the COCU description of deacons: "Deacons are baptized members of the people of God who have been ordained to represent to this people its identity in Christ as servant in the midst of the world. It belongs to diaconal ministry to struggle with the myriad needs of societies and persons—economic, political, scientific, educational, cultural, moral—in Christ's name, and so to exemplify the interdependence of worship and mission in the life of the church."[26]

Inasmuch as the Faith and Order Commission which produced the document, *Baptism, Eucharist, and Ministry,* includes among its full members Roman Catholic theologians, and in view of the fact that the Roman Catholic Church since the Second Vatican Council has produced the most comprehensive literature on the subject of the diaconate, this review of the current status of the office of deacon would be incomplete without a reference to this communion.

Although the diaconate has its roots in the New Testament, and played a very important role in the early history as well as the later development of the church of the Latin Rite, it came to be regarded primarily as a transitional step to the priesthood. As this progression in the hierarchy gradually fell into disuse because of almost universal direct ordination into the priesthood, the permanent diaconate all but disappeared. An attempt at the Council of Trent in 1563 to restore the diaconate failed and remnants of the office survived only in shadowy form until the Second Vatican Council which on September 29, 1964, approved restoration of the permanent diaconate. Nevertheless, several years were required for Rome to work out the technical implications of the approval, and not until June 18, 1967, did Pope Paul VI publish his Apostolic Letter stating the procedures required to activate the permanent diaconate. The initiative for activation is vested in episcopal conferences with the concurrence of the pope. Accordingly, Pope Paul VI approved the request of the United States Conference of Bishops in 1968, and the Bishops' Committee on the Permanent Diaconate issued guidelines in 1971 for the ministry of deacon. Since then more than 4,000 deacons have been ordained in the United States.

To facilitate the comparison of the Roman Catholic understanding of the diaconate with the understandings which have already been noted with reference to the Episcopalians and the United Methodists, as well as the ecumenical documents of the World Council of Churches' Faith and Order Commission and of the Consultation on Church Union, the address to the congregation in the Catholic Rite for the Ordination of a Deacon will be quoted in its entirety, as follows:

> This man, your relative and friend, is now to be raised to the order of deacons. Consider carefully the ministry to which he is to be promoted.
>
> He will draw new strength from the gift of the Holy Spirit. He will help the bishop and his body of priests as a minister of the word, of the altar, and of charity. He will make himself a servant of all. As a minister of the altar he will proclaim the Gospel, prepare the sacrifice, and give the Lord's body and blood to the community of believers.
>
> It will also be his duty, at the bishop's discretion, to bring God's word to believer and unbeliever alike, to preside over public prayer, to baptize, to assist at marriages and bless them, to give viaticum to the dying, and to lead the rites of burial. Once he is consecrated by the laying on of hands that comes to us from the apostles and is bound more closely to the altar, he will perform works of charity in the name of the bishop or of the pastor. From the way he goes about these duties, may you recognize him as a disciple of Jesus, who came to serve, not to be served.[27]

This address to the congregation regarding the candidates for ordination as deacon (a) again stresses the servanthood character of the office of deacon, and points to (b) the close relationship between the ministry of the altar and the ministry of charity, and (c) indicates the breadth of the deacon's responsibilities. Indeed, in the description of the deacon's duties the only basic ministerial function from which the deacon seems to be excluded is presiding at the Eucharist!

Whatever other responsibilities are assigned to deacons in the churches cited, the primary and determinative role of the diaconal ministry is that of servanthood. It is the judgment of the writer that such a remarkable unanimity should continue to shape the church's understanding of the office. This would mean that this historic form of ordained ministry should not be broadened to include those options which have been reported above as being suggested or any of the special ministries or church occupations except possibly as these options, special ministries, or occupations are clearly subsumed under the distinctive role of servant, especially to "the poor, the weak, the sick, and the lonely."

Just because a member of the household of faith happens to be *employed* by the church as secretary, parochial school teacher, or director of youth work does not remove that member from the status of laity, and as *laos* the person so employed has a recognized and valid vocation to fulfill—just as he or she would have if employed by a steel company. The place of employment does not in itself constitute sufficient reason for qualification as a candidate for the diaconate.

Nevertheless, several churches have made provision for the public recognition of laypersons ecclesiastically employed who have met certain standards for certification as professionally competent in their fields of service. Standards and procedures for certification vary from church to church, but definite progress has been made in the identification of the lay professional and in establishing such standards and procedures. Rather than attempt to generalize about the current status of lay professionals and their public recognition, the policy and program of the Lutheran Church in America will be briefly summarized as authorized and administered by the church's Division for Professional Leadership. The Division's identification of a lay professional is as follows:

> A lay professional leader in the Lutheran Church in America is a confirmed, communing, and contributing member of one of its congregations who has met the requisite educational, professional, and other standards for certification established by the Division for Professional Leadership and who is employed no less than 20 hours per week in a congregation, synod, agency, or institution of this church in a specialized area such as church educator; a

specialist in Christian education; church administrator: a specialist in administration and management, including stewardship, property, personnel, and
finance; church musician: a specialist in church music; or church worker: a
specialist in other areas, including the administration of programs and provision of services (for example, in youth ministry, in counseling, and in campus
ministry).[28]

Standards for certification include (a) commitment to the Christian
faith and to the mission and ministry of the Lutheran Church in America,
(b) knowledge and understanding of the history and teaching of the
Lutheran church, (c) completion of the appropriate educational work
either on Level I—bachelor's degree in an appropriate field or on Level
II—a master's degree in an appropriate field, (d) supervised field experience, (e) appropriate communication skills, (f) ability to relate to individuals and groups, and (g) commitment to personal and spiritual growth and
professional development.

The candidate's synod (regional unit) carries responsibility for taking
action on certification, continuation of certification, and reinstatement of
certification. A roster of certified Lay Professional Leaders is published in
the Lutheran Church in America Yearbook. In 1983 this roster included
the names of 175 persons. This number stands in striking contrast to the
9,000 clerical members of the Lutheran Church in America.

We have focused on two of the most pressing issues in the current
debate about the churches' ministry: (a) distinguishing the roles of the
clergy and the laity, and (b) extending ordination for additional functions.
Clarification if not resolution of these issues should shed light on and give
direction to the Christian's calling as service, as ministry. It is hoped that
this review of the current situation will contribute to this end.

And so we come to the end of our consideration not only of "Vocation
as Ministry" but of Christian vocation in all its meanings and manifestations. It has been the theme of these chapters that Christian vocation
makes the difference between mere existence and life transformed by the
purpose and power of God. Such is the life of every person whom the
Holy Spirit calls by the gospel, enlightens with his gifts, and sanctifies and
keeps in the true faith; even as he calls, gathers, enlightens, and sanctifies
the whole church of Christ.

God calls his children to be with him and to be with each other in his
household, the fellowship of the forgiven and the forgiving. This fellowship is known supremely in the breaking of bread together at the family

meal, in the Sacrament of the Lord's Supper. And God calls his children to service in all their relationships. After the family meal there are errands to run; the doing of tasks is the sequel to breaking bread together. For God's call gives his children both life and mission. That this gift be ours should be our constant prayer.

NOTES

1. LIFE WITHOUT VOCATION

1. Studs Terkel, *Working* (New York: Pantheon Books, 1972), p. 525.

2. Edwin J. Delattre, *The Chronicle of Higher Education*, Vol. 25, No. 17 (Jan. 5, 1983), p. 80.

3. John Oliver Nelson, ed., *Work and Vocation* (New York: Harper & Brothers, 1954), p. 142.

4. Morton Thompson, *Not as a Stranger* (New York: Charles Scribner's Sons, 1954).

5. *Time*, April 14, 1952, p. 97.

6. William H. Whyte, *The Organization Man* (New York: Doubleday & Co., 1957).

7. Ibid., chaps. 4 and 5.

8. Phillip E. Jacobs, *Changing Values in College* (New York: Harper & Brothers, 1957).

9. Arthur Levine, *When Dreams and Heroes Died: A Portrait of Today's College Student* (San Francisco: Jossey-Bass Publishers, 1980), passim, esp. p. xvii.

10. *Time*, Nov. 5, 1951.

11. Readers are referred to the comprehensive survey of workers, using the interview technique, in the volume edited by Studs Terkel to which reference has already been made.

12. The locus of this quotation cannot be identified.

13. T. S. Eliot, *The Complete Poems and Plays, 1909–1950* (New York: Harcourt, Brace & World, 1952), pp. 47–48.

14. Ibid., p. 96.

15. Nathan A. Scott, Jr., ed., *The Tragic Vision and the Christian Faith* (New York: Association Press, 1957), pp. 281–82.

16. Quoted by J. Hillis Miller, Jr., in *Tragic Vision*, ed. Scott, p. 282.

17. Scott, ed., *Tragic Vision*, p. 285.

18. Ibid., p. 291.

19. Franz Kafka, *Selected Short Stories* (New York: Modern Library, 1952), pp. 19–89.

20. J. Arthur Miller, *The Death of a Salesman* (New York: Viking Press, 1949).

21. Franz Kafka, *The Great Wall of China* (London: Secker, 1933), p. 259.

22. Ibid., p. 246.

23. Ibid., pp. 244–45.

24. Jean-Paul Sartre, *No Exit* (New York: Vintage Books, 1955), pp. 46–47.

25. Jean-Paul Sartre, *Existentialism* (New York: Philosophical Library, 1947), pp. 25–26.

26. Walter Kaufmann, ed., *Existentialism from Dostoevsky to Sartre* (New York: Meridian Books, 1956), p. 234.

27. Ignazio Silone, *Bread and Wine* (New York: Penguin Books, 1946), p. 82.

28. Walter Kaufmann, ed., *The Portable Nietzsche* (New York: Viking Books, 1954), p. 95.

29. Quoted by Nicholas Berdyaev in *The End of Our Time* (New York: Sheed & Ward, 1933), p. 72.

30. Samuel Beckett, *Waiting for Godot* (New York: Grove Press, 1954).

31. Ibid., pp. 58–59.

3. LUTHER'S UNDERSTANDING OF VOCATION

1. Eusebius, *The Proof of the Gospel*, ed. and trans. W. J. Ferrar (reprinted by Baker Book House, 1981), bk. 1, chap. 8, pp. 48, 49.

2. *The Book of Concord*, trans. and ed. Theodore G. Tappert (Philadelphia: Muhlenberg Press, 1959), p. 345.

3. Ibid., p. 419.

4. "Church Postils," in *The Precious and Sacred Writings of Martin Luther*, ed. J. N. Lenker (Minneapolis: Lutherans of All Lands Co., 1905), Vol. 10, p. 27.

5. Gustaf Wingren, *Luther on Vocation*, trans. Carl C. Rasmussen (Philadelphia: Muhlenberg Press, 1957), p. 2.

6. "Church Postils," pp. 242–43.

7. Quoted by George W. Forell in his book *Faith Active in Love* (New York: American Press, 1954), p. 148.

8. *Luther's Works*, American Edition (Philadelphia: Muhlenberg Press; and St. Louis: Concordia Publishing House, 1967), Vol. 46, p. 99. Hereafter cited as *LW*.

9. Ibid., p. 94.

10. Ibid., p. 97.

11. Ibid., Vol. 44, p. 130.

12. "Church Postils," p. 36.

13. Ibid.

14. *LW*, Vol. 31, p. 365.

15. Wingren, *Luther on Vocation*, pp. 43–44.

16. *LW,* Vol. 44, p. 71.

17. Ibid., Vol. 46, p. 223.

18. Ibid., p. 237.

19. Ibid., p. 242.

20. Ibid., p. 231.

21. Ibid., pp. 252, 253.

22. Ibid., p. 237.

23. Ibid., p. 238.

24. Ibid., p. 240.

25. Ibid., Vol. 13, p. 368.

26. Ibid.

27. "Church Postils," p. 246.

28. *Luther's Table Talk,* trans. by William Hazlitt (Philadelphia: Lutheran Publication Society, 1873), p. 447.

29. "Church Postils," p. 249.

30. *LW,* Vol. 46, p. 250.

31. Ibid., p. 229.

32. Ibid., pp. 256, 257.

33. Ibid., p. 257.

34. R. H. Tawney, *Religion and the Rise of Capitalism* (New York: Mentor Books, 1947), p. 200.

35. Max Weber, *The Protestant Ethic and the Spirit of Capitalism,* trans. by Talcott Parsons (New York: Charles Scribner's Sons, 1930).

36. George Forell, "Work and the Christian Calling," *The Lutheran Quarterly,* Vol. 8, No. 2 (May 1956): 105 – 18.

37. W. R. Forrester, *Christian Vocation* (New York: Charles Scribner's Sons, 1953), p. 154.

4. THE CALLING OF EVERYMAN TODAY

1. Harold C. Letts, ed., *Life in Community,* Christian Social Responsibility, Vol. 3 (Philadelphia: Muhlenberg Press, 1957), p. 30.

2. Ibid., p. 32.

3. *Breaking Barriers: Nairobi, 1975,* ed. David M. Paton (London: SPCK, 1975).

4. Albert Schweitzer, *J. S. Bach,* trans. Ernest Newman (London: Black, 1911), Vol. 1, pp. 166 – 67.

5. Gustaf Wingren, *Luther on Vocation,* trans. by Carl C. Rasmussen (Philadelphia: Muhlenberg Press, 1957), pp. 46 – 48.

6. Einar Billing, *Our Calling,* trans. Conrad Bergendoff (Rock Island: Augustana, 1951), p. 24.

7. Wingren, *Luther on Vocation,* p. 117.

5. VOCATION AS MINISTRY

1. *Baptism, Eucharist, and Ministry.* Faith and Order Paper No. 111 (Geneva: World Council of Churches, 1982), p. 21.

2. Hendrik Kraemer, *A Theology of the Laity* (Philadelphia: Westminster Press, 1958).

3. Hans Küng and Walter Kasper, eds., *The Plurality of Ministries* (New York: Herder and Herder, 1972), pp. 13 – 22.

4. Ibid.

5. *Baptism, Eucharist, and Ministry,* p. ix.

6. Ibid.

7. Ibid.

8. Ibid., p. 20.

9. Cf. chap. 4.

10. Ibid.

11. Ibid., pp. 27, 28.

12. Ibid., p. 22.

13. Ibid., p. 21.

14. Ibid.

15. Ibid.

16. Ibid.

17. Ibid., p. 22.

18. Ibid., p. 26.

19. Ibid., p. 27.

20. Ibid.

21. Ibid., p. 22.

22. Ibid., pp. 26, 27.

23. Ibid., p. 31.

24. *The Book of Common Prayer,* rev. ed. (New York: Oxford University Press, 1979), p. 543.

25. *A Proposed Ordinal with Introduction and Commentary for Official Alternative Use* (Board of Discipleship, United Methodist Church, 1980), pp. 30 – 31.

26. *In Quest of a Church of Christ Uniting: An Emerging Theological Consensus* (Princeton: Consultation on Church Union, revised 1980), par. 56, chap. 7.

27. *The Rites of the Catholic Church as Revised by the Second Vatican Ecumenical Council,* Vol. 2 (New York: Pueblo Publishing Co., 1980), p. 51.

28. *Lay Professional Service* (Philadelphia: Lutheran Church in America, Division for Professional Leadership, 1983).

SELECTED
BIBLIOGRAPHY

This is by no means a complete bibliography on the subject of Christian vocation. Not all publications to which reference has been made in this book have been listed. Only publications that are available in English have been included, and only a selected number of these. Attention is called to the special issues dealing with vocation and ministry of a number of magazines and journals. This brief bibliography has been prepared for those readers who wish to pursue the subject in greater depth and beyond the boundaries of this book.

Althaus, Paul. *The Ethics of Martin Luther.* Trans. with a Foreword by Robert C. Schultz. Philadelphia: Fortress Press, 1972. Esp. chaps. 3, 4, and 6.

Baptism, Eucharist, and Ministry. Faith and Order Paper No. 111. Geneva: World Council of Churches, 1982.

Beach, Waldo. *The Christian Life.* Richmond: The CLC Press, 1966. Esp. chapter 13, "Christian Vocation in an Industrial Society."

Billing, Einar. *Our Calling.* Trans. Conrad Bergendoff. Rock Island, Ill.: Augustana, 1951.

Bonhoeffer, Dietrich. *The Cost of Discipleship.* New York: Macmillan Co., 1957. Esp. chapter 3, "The Call to Discipleship."

Bucy, Ralph, ed. *The New Laity—Between Church and World.* Waco: Word Books, 1978.

Butt, Howard. *At the Edge of Hope: Christian Laity in Paradox.* New York: Seabury Press, 1978.

Calhoun, Robert C. *God and the Day's Work.* New York: Association Press, 1957.

"Calling and Jobs," Special Issue. *Katallagete,* Vol. 4, Nos. 2 – 3. Esp. Jacques Ellul, "Work and Calling," pp. 8 – 16.

Diehl, William E. *Christianity and Real Life.* Philadelphia: Fortress Press, 1978.

———. *Thank God, It's Monday.* Laity Exchange Book. Philadelphia: Fortress Press, 1982.

Empie, Paul C., and T. Austin Murphy. *Lutherans and Catholics in Dialogue IV:*

Eucharist and Ministry. Published jointly by the U.S.A. National Committee of the Lutheran World Federation and the Bishops' Committee for Ecumenical and Religious Affairs, 1970.

"Enlisting the Ministry of the Church," Special Issue. *Encounter,* Vol. 23, No. 1 (winter 1962).

"The Ethical Problem of Vocation," Special Issue. *Lutheran World,* Vol. 15, No. 2 (1968). Esp. Gustav Wingren, "The Concept of Vocation—Its Basis and Its Problems," pp. 87 – 99.

Fisher, Wallace E. *From Tradition to Mission.* New York: Abingdon Press, 1965. Chap. 6, "Living Together at Trinity," provides a good illustration of vocation within the household of faith.

——. *All the Good Gifts.* Minneapolis: Augsburg Publishing House, 1979. An up-to-date exploration of the bearing of biblical stewardship upon the corporate vocation of the Christian both within the church and as witness to the world.

Forell, George W. *Faith Active in Love.* New York: American Press, 1954. For an illuminating discussion of Luther's view of vocation in relation to "orders," see pp. 120ff.

——. "Work and the Christian Calling." *The Lutheran Quarterly,* Vol. 8, No. 2 (May 1956).

Forrester, W. R. *Christian Vocation.* New York: Charles Scribner's Sons, 1953.

Gibbs, Mark. *Christians with Secular Power.* Laity Exchange Book. Philadelphia: Fortress Press, 1976.

Gillett, Richard W. "The Reshaping of Work: A Challenge to the Churches." *The Christian Century,* Vol. 100, No. 1 (January 5 – 12, 1983).

Greenleaf, Robert K. *Servant Leadership.* New York: Paulist Press, 1977.

Hall, Cameron P. *Lay Action—The Church's Third Force.* New York: Friendship Press, 1974.

Hazelton, Roger. *God's Way with Man.* New York: Abingdon Press, 1956. Esp. chap. 7, "Technics and Vocation."

Heinecken, Martin J. "Luther and the 'Orders of Creation' in Relation to a Doctrine of Work and Vocation." *The Lutheran Quarterly,* Vol. 4, No. 4 (November 1952).

Holden, Marc. *Called by the Gospel.* Minneapolis: Augsburg Publishing House, 1983.

Holmes, Urban T., III. *The Priest in Community.* New York: Seabury Press, 1978.

Jenkins, Daniel. *Christian Maturity and Christian Success.* Laity Exchange Book. Philadelphia: Fortress Press, 1982.

Kitagawa, Joseph M. K. "Vocation and Maturity." *Criterion,* Vol. 18, No. 2 (summer 1979).

Kraemer, Hendrik. *A Theology of the Laity.* Philadelphia: Westminster Press, 1958.

Küng, Hans, and Walter Kasper, eds. *The Plurality of Ministries.* New York: Herder & Herder, 1972.

Lindbeck, George A. "The Lutheran Doctrine of the Ministry: Catholic and Reformed." *Theological Studies,* Vol. 30, No. 4 (December 1969): 588 – 612.

Luther, Martin. *Luther's Works.* American Edition, 54 vols. Philadelphia: Fortress Press; and St. Louis: Concordia Publishing House, 1955 – 75.

——. *The Precious and Sacred Writings of Martin Luther,* ed. J. N. Lenker. Minneapolis: Lutherans of All Lands Co., 1905. Attention is directed to vol. 10, *Church Postils for Advent, Christmas, and Epiphany Sermons,* which is the only complete English translation of this important material for an understanding of Luther's concept of vocation.

——. *The Table Talk of Martin Luther.* Edited by Thomas S. Kepler. New York: World Publishing Co., 1952.

——. *The Works of Martin Luther.* Philadelphia Edition, 6 vols. Philadelphia: Muhlenberg Press, 1915 – 45.

Miller, Alexander. *The Renewal of Man.* Garden City, N. Y.: Doubleday & Co., 1955. Esp. chap. 7, "The Calling of a Christian Man."

Minear, Paul S. *To Die and To Live: Christ's Resurrection and Christian Vocation.* New York: Seabury Press, 1977.

"Ministry as Vocation and Profession," Special Issue. *Dialog,* Vol. 8 (summer 1969).

Mouw, Richard J. *Called To Holy Worldliness.* Laity Exchange Book. Philadelphia: Fortress Press, 1982.

Neill, S. D., and Hans-Ruedi Weber. *The Layman in Christian History.* Philadelphia: Westminster Press, 1963.

Nelson, John Oliver, ed. *Work and Vocation.* New York: Harper & Brothers, 1954.

Nicol, Iain G. "Vocation and the People of God." *Scottish Journal of Theology,* Vol. 33 (1980): 361 – 73.

Niedner, Frederick A. "Putting On One's Neighbor: A Reading of Luther on Vocation." *Cresset,* Vol. 46, No. 7 (May 1983).

Nouwen, Henri J. M. *Creative Ministry.* New York: Doubleday & Co., 1971.

"The Pastoral Vocation," *Word and World,* Vol. 1, No. 4 (Fall 1981).

Permanent Deacons in the United States: Guidelines on Their Formation and Ministry. Washington: Bishop's Committee on the Permanent Diaconate, United States Catholic Conference, 1971.

"The Professional Ministry," Special Issue. *Quarterly Review,* Vol. 2, No. 1 (spring 1982).

Richardson, Alan. *The Biblical Doctrine of Work.* London: SCM Press, 1952.

Rulla, Luigi M. *Depth Psychology and Vocation*. Rome and Chicago: Gregorian University Press and Loyola University Press, 1971.

Schillebeeckx, Edward. *Ministry: Leadership in the Community of Jesus Christ*. New York: Crossroad, 1981.

Shelp, Earl E., and Ronald Sunderland. *A Biblical Basis for Ministry*. Philadelphia: Westminster Press, 1981.

Steere, Douglas V. *Work and Contemplation*. New York: Harper & Brothers, 1957.

Stuempfle, Herman G., Jr. *Theological and Biblical Perspectives on the Laity*. New York: Division for Mission in North America, Lutheran Church in America, 1973.

Terkel, Studs. *Working*. New York: Pantheon Books, 1972. A remarkable compendium of hundreds of interviews with all kinds of workers in the United States.

Thrall, Margaret. "Christian Vocation Today," *Theology*, Vol. 59, No. 668 (March 1976).

Torrance, T. F. *Royal Priesthood*. Edinburgh: Oliver & Boyd, 1955. A stimulating biblical study of corporate vocation in relation to the doctrine of the church and the ministry.

Wentz, Frederick K. *The Layman's Role Today*. Garden City, N.Y.: Doubleday & Co., 1963.

Wingren, Gustaf. *Luther on Vocation*. Trans. Carl C. Rasmussen. Philadelphia: Muhlenberg Press, 1957.